Myth, Literature and
the African World

Myth, Literature and the African World

WOLE SOYINKA

Professor of Comparative Literature
University of Ife, Nigeria

CAMBRIDGE UNIVERSITY PRESS

CAMBRIDGE

LONDON · NEW YORK · MELBOURNE

Published by the Syndics of the Cambridge University Press
The Pitt Building, Trumpington Street, Cambridge CB2 1RP
Bentley House, 200 Euston Road, London NW1 2DB
32 East 57th Street, New York, NY 10022, USA
296 Beaconsfield Parade, Middle Park, Melbourne 3206, Australia

First published 1976

Printed in Great Britain at the
University Printing House, Cambridge
(Euan Phillips, University Printer)

Library of Congress Cataloguing in Publication Data
Soyinka, Wole

Myth, literature and the African world.

1. African literature – History and criticism–
Addresses, essays, lectures. 2. Literature and
society – Addresses, essays, lectures. 3. Africa –
Civilization – Addresses, essays, lectures. I.
Title.

PL8010.S64   896   75-38184
ISBN 0 521 21190 5

Contents

Preface

Some details of the origination of the contents of this volume need relating as they provided an unintended (and mildly comic) pertinence to the themes of the lectures themselves. In 1973, unable to assume my position at the University of Ife, Nigeria, I accepted a year's appointment as Fellow of Churchill College, Cambridge. I was simultaneously Visiting Professor at Sheffield University, at which institution I came directly into the Department of English which boasts a full African Literature programme, including a course leading to a post-graduate degree. Cambridge was somewhat more circumspect. On the initiative of the Department of Social Anthropology, a series of lectures on Literature and Society was proposed in which the Department of English was, naturally, to participate. The idea turned out to be not so natural. The lectures were duly given, but they took place entirely in the Department of Social Anthropology. Casual probing after it was all over indicated that the Department of English (or perhaps some key individual) did not believe in any such mythical beast as 'African Literature'. A student of mine whose post-graduate project was centred on mythopoeia in black literature had apparently undergone a similar experience before the approval of his subject. If I had not, providentially, been available as his tutor, it seemed likely that the lack of adequate supervision would have become a key argument in the rejection of his proposed programme.

I was, paradoxically, quite sympathetic to the dilemma of the English Literature traditionalists. They at least have not gone so far as to deny the existence of an African world – only its literature and, perhaps, its civilisation. Many African universities have begun to reconsider the once convenient location of contemporary African literature as an appendage of English literature. A few have sensibly substituted the title Department of (Comparative) Literature for the orthodox Department of English. Others have, not so satisfactorily, brought the study of African literature under a Department of African Studies. Important as it sounds, however, the problem of nomenclature is ultimately secondary, the motivation being everything. Today this goes beyond the standard anti-colonial purge of learning and education and embraces the apprehension of a culture whose reference points are taken from within the culture itself. The themes which were selected for these lectures are a reflection of this positive apprehension.

It is often difficult to convey, both to aliens and to the alienated within one's society, the replete reality of this self-apprehension. Social emancipation, cultural liberation, cultural revolution are easier but deflective approaches, for they all retain external reference points against which a progression in thinking can be measured. The expression of a true self-apprension is itself still most accessible today in the active language of cultural liberation etc.; that is, in order to transmit the self-apprehension of a race, a culture, it is sometimes necessary to liberate from, and relate this collective awareness to, the values of others. The misunderstanding of this merely expedient process is what in African academia has created a deified aura around what is falsely called intellectualism (= knowledge and exposition of the reference points of colonial cultures). To the truly self-apprehending entity within the African world reality, this amounts to intellectual bondage and self-betrayal.

Having contested the claims of Negritude since my earliest contact with its exegetes, a position which is still affirmed in the trend of these lectures, a contradiction may appear in their emphasis, which is one of eliciting the African self-apprehended world in myth and literature. These positions are, I hope, clarified in the lectures and demonstrated to be not only mutually compatible but consistently so. The choice of the theme is of course not fortuitous. I have long been preoccupied with the process of apprehending my own world in its full complexity, also through its contemporary progression and distortions – evidence of this is present both in my creative work and in one of my earliest essays, *The Fourth Stage,* included in this collection as an appendix. The persistent thread in the more recent lectures stems from this earliest effort to encapsulate my understanding of this metaphysical world and its reflection in Yoruba contemporary social psyche. *The Fourth Stage* was in fact published in its first and only draft – I was arrested and became incommunicado soon after I sent it to the editor, requesting him to pass it on to G. Wilson Knight, my former Professor at Leeds, for his comments. I have tried now to reduce what a student of mine complained of as 'elliptical' obstacles to its comprehension. There were in addition a number of printing (or typing) errors which further obstructed clarity – these have been removed. The essays on drama will be seen as more recent elaborations of this central concern to transmit through analysis of myth and ritual the self-apprehension of the African world.

There has however developed in recent years (especially in the last four or five) a political reason for this increased obsession with the particular theme. From a well-publicised position as an anti-Negritudinist (if only one knew in advance what would make one statement more memorable than the next!) it has been with an increasing sense of alarm and even betrayal that we have watched our position distorted and exploited to embrace a 'sophisticated' school of thought which (for ideological reasons) actually repudiates the existence of an African world! Both in cultural and political publications, and at such encounters as the UNESCO Conference on the Influence of Colonialism on African Culture, Dar es Salaam 1972, the 6th Pan-African Congress, Dar es Salaam 1974, the pre-Colloque of the Black Arts Festival, Dakar 1974 etc., etc., we black Africans have been blandly invited to submit ourselves to a second epoch of colonisation – this time by a universal-humanoid abstraction defined and conducted by individuals whose theories and prescriptions are derived from the apprehension of *their* world and *their* history, *their* social neuroses and *their* value systems. It is time, clearly, to respond to this new threat, each in his own field. The whoring profession which the practice of literary criticism sometimes suggests will hopefully play its part in this contest whose timing, when we recall that we are at a definitive stage of African self-liberation, is particularly crucial. For after (or simultaneously with) an externally-directed and conclusive confrontation on the continent must come a reinstatement of the values authentic to that society, modified only by the demands of a contemporary world. This appears an obvious enough process in the schemata of interrupted histories. Could this be why of late we Africans have been encountering a concerted assault, decked in ideological respectability, on every attempt to re-state the authentic world of the African peoples and ensure its contemporary apprehension through appropriate structures? In vain we conjure with the names of Mbiti, Bolaji Idowu, Ogotommeli, Kagame, Willie Abrahams, Cheik Anta Diop, and foreign triers like Father Tempels, Pierre Verger, Herskovits etc. For the new breed of deniers they have never existed nor written a line, nor provided one clue that fleshes out, at the very least, a composite image of the African world.

The Yoruba have a proverb for it: its wit is unfortunately lost in translation, being based on a pun on *'ni*

tan (related to each other) and *n'ítan* (at the thigh): *A ò lè
b'ára 'ni tan, k'á f'ara wa n'ítan ya.* A free translation
would read: Kinship does not insist that, because we are
entwined, we thereby rip off each other's thigh. The man
who, because of ideological kinship tries to sever my
being from its self-apprehension is not merely culturally
but politically hostile. (Trotsky understood this only too
well, so did Amilcar Cabral.) When ideological relations
begin to deny, both theoretically and in action, the
reality of a cultural entity which we define as the African
world while asserting theirs even to the extent of inviting
the African world to sublimate its existence in theirs, we
must begin to look seriously into their political motivation. This volume does not however concern itself with
that. It is engaged in what should be the simultaneous
act of eliciting from history, mythology and literature, for
the benefit of both genuine aliens and alienated Africans,
a continuing process of self-apprehension whose temporary dislocation appears to have persuaded many of
its non-existence or its irrelevance (= retrogression, reac-
tionarism, racism, etc.) in contemporary world reality.

Some of the literature discussed in these lectures has
a note of stridency; this in itself is an index of the sudden
awakening of a new generation of writers to threats to
their self-apprehension. Such writers are, without exception, those who have responded with boredom and
indifference to the romanticised rhetoric of Negritude.
The stridency in their voices is a predictable reaction to
the experience of being stabbed in the back, and from
totally unexpected quarters. To refuse to participate in
the creation of a new cult of the self's daily apprehended
reality is one thing; to have that reality contemptuously
denied or undermined by other cultic adherents is far
more dangerous and arouses extreme reactions. The
solution, for the moment, appears to be a continuing
objective re-statement of that self-apprehension, to call
attention to it in living works of the imagination, placing

them in the context of primal systems of apprehension of the race.

Nothing in these essays suggests a detailed uniqueness of the African world. Man exists, however, in a comprehensive world of myth, history and mores; in such a total context, the African world, like any other 'world' is unique. It possesses, however, in common with other cultures, the virtues of complementarity. To ignore this simple route to a common humanity and pursue the alternative route of negation is, for whatever motives, an attempt to perpetuate the external subjugation of the black continent. There is nothing to choose ultimately between the colonial mentality of an Ajayi Crowther, West Africa's first black bishop, who grovelled before his white missionary superiors in a plea for patience and understanding of his 'backward, heathen, brutish' brothers, and the new black ideologues who are embarrassed by statements of self-apprehension by the new 'ideologically backward' African. Both suffer from externally induced fantasies of redemptive transformation in the image of alien masters. Both are victims of the doctrine of self-negation, the first requirement for a transcendentalist (political or religious) fulfilment. Like his religious counterpart, the new ideologue has never stopped to consider whether or not the universal verities of his new doctrine are already contained in, or can be elicited from the world-view and social structures of his own people. The study of much contemporary African writing reveals that they can: this group of literature I have described as the literature of a secular social vision. It marks the beginning of a prescriptive validation of an African self-apprehension.

W.S.

Accra
September 1975

1

Morality and aesthetics
in the ritual archetype

I shall begin by commemorating the gods for their
self-sacrifice on the altar of literature, and in so doing
press them into further service on behalf of human
society, and its quest for the explication of being. I have
selected three paradigms. The number is purely fortuitous; there is no intent to create a literary trinity, holy
or unholy – their choice is governed by the nature of
their attributes which, in addition to their manipulable
histories, have made them the favourites of poets and
dramatists, modern and traditional. In addition (and this
of course is true for many of their companion deities),
they appear to travel well. The African world of the
Americas testifies to this both in its socio-religious reality
and in the secular arts and literature. Symbols of Yemaja
(Yemoja), Oxosi (Ososi), Exu (Esu) and Xango (Sango)
not only lead a promiscuous existence with Roman
Catholic saints but are fused with the twentieth-century
technological and revolutionary expressionism of the
mural arts of Cuba, Brazil and much of the Caribbean.

The three deities that concern us here are Ogun,
Obatala and Sango. They are represented in drama by
the passage-rites of hero-gods, a projection of man's
conflict with forces which challenge his efforts to har-
monise with his environment, physical, social and psychic. The drama of the hero-god is a convenient
expression; gods they are unquestionably, but their symbolic roles are identified by man as the role of an
intermediary quester, an explorer into territories of
'essence-ideal' around whose edges man fearfully skirts.
Finally, as a prefiguration of conscious being which is

I

nevertheless a product of the conscious creativity of man, they enhance man's existence within the cyclic consciousness of time. These emerge as the principal features of the drama of the gods; it is within their framework that traditional society poses its social questions or formulates its moralities. They control the aesthetic considerations of ritual enactment and give to every performance a multi-level experience of the mystical and the mundane.

The setting of Ritual, of the drama of the gods, is the cosmic entirety, and our approach to this drama might usefully be made through the comparable example of the Epic which represents also, on a different level, another access to the Rites of Passage. The epic celebrates the victory of the human spirit over forces inimical to self-extension. It concretises in the form of action the arduous birth of the individual or communal entity, creates a new being through utilising and stressing the language of self-glorification to which human nature is healthily prone. The dramatic or tragic rites of the gods are, however, engaged with the more profound, more elusive phenomenon of being and non-being. Man can shelve and even overwhelm metaphysical uncertainties by epic feats, and prolong such a state of social euphoria by their constant recital, but this exercise in itself proves a mere surrogate to the bewildering phenomenon of the cosmic location of his being. The fundamental visceral questioning intrudes, prompted by the patient, immovable and eternal immensity that surrounds him. We may speculate that it is the reality of this undented vastness which created the need to challenge, confront and at least initiate a rapport with the realm of infinity. It was – there being no other conceivable place – the natural home of the unseen deities, a resting-place for the departed, and a staging-house for the unborn. Intuitions, sudden psychic emanations could come, logically, only from such an incomparable immensity. A chthonic realm, a storehouse for creative and destructive essences, it required a challenger, a human representative to breach it periodically on behalf of the well-being of the community. The stage, the ritual arena of confrontation, came to represent the symbolic chthonic space and the presence of the challenger within it is the earliest physical expression of man's fearful awareness of the cosmic context of his existence. Its magic microcosm is created by the communal presence, and in this charged space the chthonic inhabitants are challenged.

This context however is the cosmic *totality,* in speaking of which it must be constantly recalled that we do not excise that portion of it which, because so readily and physically apprehended, tends to occupy a separate (mundane) category in modern European imagination. This was not always so. This gradual erosion of Earth in European metaphysic scope is probably due to the growth and influence of the Platonic–Christian tradition. After all, the pagan Greek did not neglect this all-important dimension. Persephone, Dionysos and Demeter were terrestrial deities. Pluto not merely ruled but inhabited the netherworld. Neptune was a very watery god who conducted his travels on water-spouts. Those archetypal protagonists of the chthonic realm, Orpheus, Gilgamesh, Ulysses, did penetrate this netherworld in concrete and elemental terms. And before that oriental twin-brother of Christianity – Buddhism – attenuated and circumscribed Asiatic thought, Lord Shiva drove his passionate course through earth, uniting all the elements with his powerful erection which burst through to the earth's surface, split in three and spurted sperm in upper cosmos. In Asian and European antiquity, therefore, man did, like the African, exist within a cosmic totality, did possess a consciousness in which his own earth being, his gravity-bound apprehension of self, was inseparable from the entire cosmic phenomenon. (For let it always be recalled that myths arise from man's attempt to externalise and communicate his inner intuitions.) A

3

profound transformation has therefore taken place within the human psyche if, to hypothesise, the same homo sapiens mythologises at one period that an adventurous deity has penetrated earth, rocks and underground streams with his phallus, going right through into the outer atmosphere, and, at another period, that a new god walks on water without getting his feet wet. The latter hints already at cosmic Manichaeism, evidence of which we shall encounter in the aesthetic structure of the drama of African deities in their new syncretic abode across the Atlantic. The seed of anti-terrestrialism sowed by Buddhism and Judeo-Christianity had to end with such excesses as the transference of the underworld to a new locale up in the sky, a purgatorial suburb under the direct supervision of the sky deities. The multiple epiphanous deities have become for the European a thing of distant memory, and heroes who once dared the divine monopoly of the chthonic realm fade into dubious legend. The ultimate consequence of this – in terms of man's cosmic condition – is that the cosmos recedes further and further until, while retaining something of the grandeur of the infinite, it loses the essence of the tangible, the immediate, the appeasable. It moves from that which can be tangibly metaphorphosed into realms of the fantasied; commencing *somewhere else,* where formerly it began, co-existed with, and was completed within the reality of man's physical being and environment. Thus, where formerly the rites of the exploration of the chthonic realm, of birth and re-birth, the rites of regress and entry, were possible from any one of the various realms of existence into any other, for and on behalf of any being – ancestor, living, or unborn – living man now restricted his vision of existence to the hierarchic circuits immediately above earth. Ritual drama, that is drama as a cleansing, binding, communal, re-creative force, disappears or is vitiated during such periods or within such cultures which survive only by the narrowing of the cosmic whole. It is instructive to observe the commencement of this process in the drama of the gods in contemporary Christian-influenced societies of the African world.

To speak of space, music, poetry or material paraphernalia in the drama of the gods is to move directly from the apparent to deeper effects within the community whose drama (that is history, morality, affirmation, supplication, thanksgiving or simple calendrification) it also is. This is not to suggest that such drama *always* operates on this level. Casual secular entertainment may also involve the gods – the gods are quite amenable to fustian, nowhere more so than in their most sacred *oriki* (praise-chants) – but such pieces do not concern themselves with creating the emotional and spiritual overtones that would pervade, as a matter of course, the consecrated spot where the divine presence must be invoked and borne within the actor-surrogate.

This brings us briefly to the question of art. The difficulty of today's agent of a would-be ritual communication (call him the producer) is that, where the drama of the gods is involved, his sensibility is more often than not that of an enthusiastic promoter, very rarely that of a truly communicant medium in what is essentially a 'rite of passage'. To move from its natural habitat in the shrine of the deity, or a historic spot in the drama of a people's origin, or a symbolic patch of earth amidst grain stalks on the eve of harvest; to move from such charged spaces to a fenced arena at a Festival of Arts, or even to an authentic shelter of the god only lately adapted for tourists and anthropologists alike; this constitutes an unfair strain on the most even-tempered deity, and also on the artistic temperament he shares with humanity. This is not simply a question of truncation, such as the removal of the more sacred events from profane eyes. The essential problem is that the emotive progression

5

which leads to a communal ecstacy or catharsis has been destroyed in the process of re-staging. So this leads us intentionally to the perennial question of whether ritual can be called drama, at what moment a religious or mythic celebration can be considered transformed into drama, and whether the ultimate test of these questions does not lie in their capacity to transfer from habitual to alien environments.

These questions are as frequently posed as they are largely artificial. The anguish over what is ritual and what drama has indeed been rendered even more abstract by the recent reversion of European and American progressive theatre to ritualism in its 'purest' attainable form. This is especially true of the black theatre in America but is also true of the current white avant-garde in Europe and America. How, except as a groping towards the ritual experience (alas, only too often comically misguided) could we describe the theatrical manifestations of the so-called 'Liquid Theatre' or the more consciously anthropological 'Environmental Theatre' in America? Or the intense explorations of Grotowski into the human psyche? What more concise expression could capture the spirit of the spectacle mounted by the French director Mnouchkine in her *1789* other than a 'ritual of revolution'? Peter Brook's experiments which took his company to Persepolis for a production of *Orghast,* a play in a wholly invented non-language, are propelled by this same need to re-discover the origin, the root experience of what Western European man later reduced to specialist terminologies through his chronic habit of compartmentalisation. (It is by the way a very catching habit; we have all caught it to some extent.) Their modern forerunner (European that is) was of course Jean Genêt, but his drama only revealed a potential for the eventual distillation of a heavily literary theatre into pure ritualistic essence. It is no surprise that towards the close of the sixties, the company which created a New York version of Euripides' *Bacchae* should draw, among other sources, upon an Asmat New Guinea ritual in its search for the tragic soul of twentieth-century white bourgeois–hippie American culture. The question therefore of the supposed dividing line between ritual and theatre should not concern us much in Africa, the line being one that was largely drawn by the European analyst. Groups such as the Ori-Olokun Theatre in Ife, and Duro Ladipo's company, also of Nigeria, have demonstrated the capability of the drama (or ritual) of the gods to travel as aesthetically and passionately as the gods themselves have, across the Atlantic. So indeed have groups in black America, such as Barbara Ann Teer's Harlem Theatre. If civil servants (beginning with the colonial administrators) and even university entrepreneurs who are most often responsible for bringing our Cultural Heritage out of its wraps to regale foreign delegations, Institute of African Studies conferences etc., retain the basic attitude that traditional drama is some kind of village craft which can be plonked down on any stall just like artifacts in any international airport boutique, it should not surprise us that the spectator sums up his experience as having been entertained or bored by some 'quaint ritual'. Such presentations have been largely responsible for the multitude of false concepts surrounding the drama of the gods; that, and their subjection to anthropological punditry where they are reduced, *in extremis,* to behavioural manifestations in primitive society. The burden on a producer is one of knowledge, understanding, and of sympathetic imagination. Whatever deity is involved demands an intelligent communication of what is, indeed, pure essence.

Now let us speak of the gods and of their fates – both in myth and at the hands of their creative exploiters.

Sango, of whom more will be said in chapter 2, interests us here only in respect of his essentiality, which enables us to relate him to a cosmic functionalist framework, in

company with several deities. This description 'functionalist' does not imply that other deities such as Ogun
and Obatala with whom he is later contrasted do not also
fulfil functionalist roles in the Yoruba man–cosmos
organisation. The distinction is largely one of degree, or
emphasis: in what primary sense a deity is thought upon
in a community of his worshippers, the affective ends
towards which he is most readily invoked. In Sango's
case, it is as the agency of lightning, lightning in turn
being the cosmic instrument of a swift, retributive
justice.

Sango is anthropomorphic in origin, but it is necessary,
in attempting to enter fully into the matrix of a society's
conceptions of becoming, to distinguish between the
primary and secondary paradigms of origin – the primal
becoming of man, and his racial or social origination.
Sango is cast in the latter frame, and his tragic rites are
consequently a deadly conflict on the human and historic
plane, charged nonetheless with the passion and terror
of superhuman, uncontrollable forces. Duro Ladipo's
play *Oba Koso* will be discussed more fully in another
context, but some apposite lines from the Brazilian Zora
Zeljan's play on Oxala (Orisa-nla) in which Sango features prominently will convey some of the awesome
passion of the man. After dearth, famine and plagues,
caused by a crime of injustice against a disguised deity,
committed within his kingdom but without his knowledge, Sango at last discovers the identity of the long-
suffering god. In rage, he challenges Olodumare, the
Supreme Deity:

> Blow, winds, and efface the memory of this crime!
> Swell seas, and wash my kingdom clean of this guilt!
> And you, lord of destiny, how can I respect you
> from now on? You wrote my life in the eternal
> books. You are to blame for it! Thunders that I
> control, explode with all your might! Attack the

heavens! I want to fight with Olodumare. I
challenge that power which made me cover myself
with so much shame! More! More! More! Set fire to
the skies![1]

He is brought under control only by Oxala, the victim
of the original injustice, who rebukes Sango's blasphemy.
Yet Sango's rage is wholly understandable and reinforces
a clever philosophical issue deployed by Zora Zeljan to
reinforce the essence of Sango as the principle of justice.
Since the crime against the disguised deity was committed in his own land, Sango has to bear responsibility for
it; yet he is innocent of the crime. Zora Zeljan's dramatic
shrewdness lay in basing the motivation for Sango's
passion, not on the unfairness of the long curse on his
land, but on the egotistical realisation that he, Sango,
principle of justice itself, had been unwittingly made to
commit an unjust act. His reaction, terrible and blasphe-
mous as it is, raises him to truly superhuman, super-
daemonic levels. It is doubtful if any philosopher would
want to raise, confronted with this spectacle of passion,
the finer points of the principles of culpability. Sango
embodies in his person, in that culminating moment, the
awesome essence of justice; nor is it disputable that the
achievement of this is in large measure due to the
ritualist mould of the play, where all action and all
personae reach deeply through reserves of the collective
memory of human rites of passage – ordeal, survival,
social and individual purgation – into an end result
which is the moral code of society.

Sometimes, in the historic pattern of Sango's rites,
there appears to be a temporal dislocation. I have stressed that Sango's history is not the history of primal
becoming but of racial origin, which is historically dated.
Yet he leaps straight after his suicide (or non-suicide,
to be liturgically correct) into an identification (by

[1] Zora Zeljan, *Oxala, Transition* no. 47 (1974), p. 31.

implication) with the source of lightning. This seeming
cosmic anachronism is in fact a very handy clue to
temporal concepts in the Yoruba world-view. Traditional
thought operates, not a linear conception of time but a
cyclic reality. One does not suggest for a moment that
this is peculiar to the Yoruba or to the African world-view.
Kerenyi elicits parallel verities from Greek mythology in
his essay 'The primordial child in primordial times'.[2] But
the degree of integrated acceptance of this temporal
sense in the life-rhythm, mores and social organisation
of Yoruba society is certainly worth emphasising, being
a reflection of that same reality which denies periodicity
to the existences of the dead, the living and the unborn.
The expression 'the child is father of the man' becomes,
within the context of this time-structure, not merely a
metaphor of development, one that is rooted in a system
of representative individuation, but a proverb of human
continuity which is not uni-directional. Neither 'child'
nor 'father' is a closed or chronological concept. The
world of the unborn, in the Yoruba world-view, is as
evidently older than the world of the living as the world
of the living is older than the ancestor-world. And, of
course, the other way around: we can insist that the world
of the unborn is older than the world of the ancestor in
the same breath as we declare that the deities preceded
humanity into the universe. But there again we come up
against the Yoruba proverb: *Bi o s'enia, imale o si* (if
humanity were not, the gods would not be). Hardly a
companionable idea to the Judeo-Christian theology of
'In the beginning, God *was*', and of course its implications go beyond the mere question of sequential time.
Whatever semantic evasion we employ – the godness,
the beingness of god, the otherness of, or assimilate
oneness with god – they remain abstractions of man-

[2] In C. G. Jung and C. Kerenji, *Introduction to a Science of
Mythology,* translated by R. F. C. Hull, Routledge & Kegan Paul,
London, 1970.

emanating concepts or experiences which presuppose the human medium. No philosophy or ontological fanaticism can wish that away, and it is formulative of Yoruba cosmogonic wisdom. It is also an affective social principle which intertwines multiple existences so absolutely that, to take a common enough example, an elderly man would refer to a child as *Baba* (father, or elder) if the circumstances of his birth made his actual entry into the living world retrospective. His conduct towards the child would be so deferential that he might never call him by his real name. If he held a family feast, the elder's place of honour would go to the child-guest. It is a balancing principle, one which prevents total inflexibility in the age-hierarchies which normally govern traditional society.

The deities exist in the same relation with humanity as these multiple worlds and are an expression of its cyclic nature. Sango's fusion with a primal phenomenon is an operation of the same concept, and the drama on a human plane that precedes his apotheosis is a further affirmation of the principle of continuity inherent in myths of origin, secular or cosmic. Sango's 'tragic fall' is the result of a hubristic act: the powerful king throws himself in conflict not simply with subjects or peers but with the racial fount of his own being. Weak, vacillating, treacherous and disloyal, the human unit that constitutes the chorus of his downfall is, in Sango's drama, the total context of racial beginning; the ritual metaphor communicates this and the poetry is woven into its affirmation. Yet side by side with acceptance of the need to destroy this disruptive, uncontrollable factor in the mortal community, the need to assert the communal will for a harmonious existence, is recognition of the superhuman energies of an exceptional man. Apotheosis, the joining of energies in cosmic continuity, follows logically; and Sango is set to work at his new functions with a wide safety zone of ether between him and lesser mortals.

Of course we may also, like Paul Radin, be justified in seeing this act of apotheosis in the opportunistic light of the self-entrenching priesthood.[3] Duro Ladipo's play *Oba Koso*[4] indicates quite clearly that Sango did commit suicide, that it was the priests who got quickly together, hushed the wailing of the women and rebuked them for revealing that Sango took his own life. The body conveniently disappears and his elevation is attested: The king is dead; long live the god! And why not indeed? Economics and power have always played a large part in the championing of new deities throughout human history. The struggle for authority in early human society with its prize of material advantages, social prestige and the establishment of an elite has been nowhere so intensely marked as in the function of religion, perpetuating itself in repressive orthodoxies, countered by equally determined schisms. In the exploration of man's images of essence-ideal, fashioned in the shape of gods, we cannot afford to jettison our cynical faculties altogether. Adapting *The Bacchae* of Euripides quite recently for a production – *The Bacchae* is of course the finest extant drama of the social coming-into-being of a semi-European deity – I found it necessary to emphasise this impure aspect of the priesthood. There is a confrontation between King Pentheus who is properly opposed to the presence and activities of the god Dionysus in his kingdom, and the seer Tiresias who is already an enthusiastic promoter of the god. Here are a few lines from King Pentheus' denunciation:

> This is your doing Tiresias; I know
> You talked him into it, and I know why.
> Another god revealed is a new way opened
> Into men's pockets, profits from offerings,
> Power over private lives – and state affairs –

[3] Paul Radin, *Primitive Religion; its Nature and Origin,* Dover, New York, 1957.

[4] Duro Ladipo, *Three Yoruba Plays,* Heinemann, London, 1973.

The ritual archetype

Don't deny it! I've known your busy priesthood
Manipulations.

It seemed only fair to give Pentheus a persuasive dissent-
ing view, the view of state authority in conflict with an
imagined theocratic conspiracy since, as he is to learn so
tragically, he happens to be wrong. Of course it is quite
possible to re-create the Sango myth from this basic
viewpoint; indeed, Duro Ladipo's play would provide a
good beginning. The result would hardly be ritual,
however. The narration of a moment in the history of
the Oyo, even a tragic conflict involving their first king,
might result from it, but not the drama of the gods as
a medium of communal recollection and cohesion, not
the consolation which comes from participating in the
process of bringing to birth a new medium in the cosmic
extension of man's physical existence.

We now turn to Obatala, a gentler sector of the arc of
the human psyche (to keep within that cyclic image of
Yoruba existential concepts). Within his crescent is stored
those virtues of social and individual accommodation:
patience, suffering, peaceableness, all the imperatives of
harmony in the universe, the essence of quietude and
forbearance; in short, the aesthetics of the saint. On the
very far side of such an arc we find the protagonist
assertiveness of Ogun, our third deity. Common to all
these gods, it may be remarked at this point, is that even
when, like Obatala, they bear the essence of purity, their
history is always marked by some act of excess, hubris
or other human weakness. The consequences are, significantly, measured in human terms and such gods are
placed under an eternal obligation of some practical
form of penance which compensates humanity. Since the
resemblance of the Greek pantheon to the Yoruba is
often remarked, leading even in some instances of strong
scholarly nerve to 'conclusive evidence' for the thesis that

the Yoruba religion is derived from the Greek, it is instructive to point out a fundamental contrast. Like the Yoruba deities, but to a thousandfold degree, the Greek gods also commit serious infractions against mortal well-being. The Greek catalogue is one of lust, greed, sadism, megalomania and sheer cussedness. But the morality of reparation appears totally alien to the ethical concepts of the ancient Greeks. Punishments, when they occur among the Olympians, invariably take place only when the offence happens to encroach on the mortal preserves of another deity and that deity is stronger or successfully appeals to Father Zeus, the greatest reprobate of all. And of course it was commonly accepted that the rape, mutilation, or death of a mortal minion of the offending deity could go some way towards settling the score to the satisfaction of all. This is the ethical basis of Greek tragedy, not as it began in the ritual *tragodia* but as it developed through the pessimistic line of Aeschylus to Shakespeare's

> As flies to wanton boys, are we to the gods;
> They kill us for their sport.   (*King Lear*)

The psychological base – the 'tragic flaw' in the hero – was a later refinement; Oedipus the Innocent remained the ethical archetype of Greek tragedy.

That Greek religion shows persuasive parallels with, to stick to our example, the Yoruba is by no means denied; the Delphic Oracle and the Ifa Corpus of the Yoruba are a fascinating instance of one such structural parallel. But the essential differences in the actual autochthonous myths of the gods themselves provide clues to differences in the moral bias of the two world-views. The penalties which societies exact from their deities in reparation for real or symbolic injuries are an index of the extent to which the principles of *natural* restitution for social disharmony may be said to govern the moral structure of that society and influence its social laws – a *natural* restitution, because the relationship between man and god (embodiment of nature and cosmic principles) cannot be seen in any other terms but that those of naturalness. This relationship represents the deductions and applications of cosmic and natural ordering, and it is not only ethical but technical (for instance, economic) norms which they provide for such a society. By making the gods responsible to judgements so based, a passive reliance on the whims of external forces is eschewed, their regenerative aspects are catalysed into operation through a ritual recourse to the gods' error-ridden rites of passage. Even in the corpus of Ifa curative verse we encounter constant references to such antecedents in divine moral history. Divine memory is not permitted to rest and prayers are uttered as reminders of natural responsibilities. Of course, it must be admitted that the actualities of the continent today reveal no such awareness to the observer. The saying *orisa l'oba,* (the king is a god), embraced at a superficial self-gratifying level, fails to recall today's power-holders to the moral nature of the African deity. The leaders' mentality is decidedly Olympian, their gods are Greek. Yet it is from their lips that is most often heard the boast of indigenous authenticity. The African deities must be chuckling in their abodes – except perhaps Obatala the saint.

The uncancelled error of Obatala, god of soul purity, was his weakness for drink. To him belongs the function of moulding human beings, into whose forms life is breathed by the supreme deity himself, Olodumare. One day, however, Obatala allowed himself to take a little too much of that potent draught, palm wine. His craftsman's fingers slipped badly and he moulded cripples, albinos and the blind. As a result of this error, Obatala rigidly forbids palm wine to his followers. (Part of the compensating principle of the Yoruba world-view is revealed in the fact that by contrast, Ogun, who was yet another victim of the draught, makes palm wine a mandatory ingredient of his worship. The Yoruba can be reassuringly pragmatic. Unless one is in the unfortunate position of being actually marked for priesthood in the worship of Obatala it is possible still to be a sincere follower of that deity, stay ecstatically sober at his outing, then wind up the festival of the gods by getting beatifically drunk on Ogun's day.) Obatala's day of error is occasionally but not consistently given as a contributory factor to the necessity of his rites of passage. It emerges as a drama of his spiritual essence through capture, ordeal, ransoming, and triumphal return – a passion play which is linked to the dearth-and-plenty cycle of nature.

Two plays are of particular interest in the drama of this god; one by Obotunde Ijimere is titled *The Imprisonment of Obatala*.[5] The other is by the Brazilian Zora Zeljan. Entitled *The Story of Oxala* and subtitled *The Feast of Bomfin,* on which Brazilian feast it is based, the play testifies directly to the vitality of African religions in Latin America and the Caribbean.[6] Oxala is the Brazilian corruption of the name Orisa-nla, which is another name by which Obatala is known among the Yoruba. In the prologue to her play, Zora Zeljan writes:

> The Feast of Bomfin, in Bahia, is one of the best examples of religious syncretism in our times. It is a compound of Catholic saints and African orisas, which testifies to the conciliatory spirit of mixed civilizations. That is why the Feast of Bomfin is also the story of Oxala. The play originates in one of the legends of Oxala, the god that the candomble believers have syncretised with our Lord of Bomfin. In the process of being catechised, the slaves embodied the new idea of Christ's Passion with their ancestral memory of Oxala's captivity. He was the

[5] Obotunde Ijimere, *The Imprisonment of Obatala and other plays,* Heinemann, London, 1966.
[6] *Transition* no. 47 (1974).

father of all the other gods in their theogony. In a sort of penance, and echoing customs whose origins were buried in time, the uncomplicated piety of the Brazilian Negroes induced in them a desire to expiate a racial burden. It was as if they wanted to relive the sorrow of their main deity, a sort of compensation and restitution of his figure to its former majesty and dignity. (*Oxala,* p. 33)

There are, of course, a few points to quarrel with in that: the concept of expiating a racial burden is something which has been taken over from Judeo-Christianity. Compensation and restitution are natural enough goals for an enslaved race in those circumstances, but expiation of a racial burden is pure racial transposition by the guilty. Nothing, especially in the rebellious history of the slaves in Brazil, can uphold this interpretation which is a reflection of the European conscience.

A determination to replant the displaced racial psyche was one reason for the ease and permanence with which the African gods were syncretised with Roman Catholic saints. The process was so complete that these deities became part of the spiritual lives of the white Roman Catholics themselves who, in Brazil or Cuba, became regular worshippers in the *candomble* or *bembe* (the respective Brazilian and Cuban terms) adopting the Yoruba orisa in their full essence as their patron gods. One interesting point I ought to mention, as it is related to the actual course of action in Zeljan's play: she remarks in her introduction that while she obtained the story of Oxala's tragic wanderings from Pierre Verger's *Dieux d'Afrique,* she found in that book no reference to the motives which made Oxala face Destiny in that form. These motives were later gradually clarified for her through legends with which she came into contact in Rio or Bahia, and they had to be re-assembled as they had become appended to several other legends to which they did not belong. And the remote causes which Zeljan uncovered in Brazil and assigns to Oxala's journey not only differ from those of Obotunde Ijimere and Yoruba traditional lore, but offer us, by contrast, a significant piece in the fabric of Yoruba metaphysics. Zora Zeljan makes Sango journey in pursuit of his wife Nana Buruku, who has deserted him. And in the reasons for her desertion and Oxala's defence we find where Christian god-attributes differ from the Yoruba. We learn from the Brazilian that Oxala made a son for himself called 'Omolu', lord of the Earth. Since he was to be the curative god, with power over illness and health, life and death, Oxala made him ugly and sick in his own flesh. So disgusted was Nana Buruku who gave birth to him that she threw him into an abyss where, in addition to the deformities from which he was already suffering, he also developed a club foot. When, to add insult to injury, Oxala gave her a second son, Exu, who was created indifferent to the principles of good and evil, she fled him and took refuge in Sango's kingdom, swearing never to return.

We see how, in contrast to the Yoruba assertion of moments of weakness and general shortcomings in the god in the performance of his functions, Christian syncretism in Bahia rationalises the existence of the malformed in human society within the overall framework of farsightedness and supra-human understanding of the creator god. The Yoruba assert straightforwardly that the god was tipsy and his hand slipped, bringing the god firmly within the human attribute of fallibility. Since human fallibility is known to entail certain disharmonious consequences for society, it also requires a search for remedial activities, and it is this cycle which ensures the constant regenerative process of the universe. By bringing the gods within this cycle, a continuity of cosmic regulation involving the worlds of the ancestor and the unborn is also guaranteed. The act of hubris or

its opposite – weakness, excessive passivity or inertia –
leads to a disruption of balances within nature and this
in turn triggers off compensating energies.

The action in both versions – Zora Zeljan's and Ijimere's – follows a near-identical pattern, apart from the
motivation. Oxala undertakes the journey into Xango's
kingdom, is molested on the way by Esu the trickster god
and subjected to a hundred humiliations. He bears all
patiently. He is imprisoned (once again through Esu's
machinations) on a false charge of stealing the king's
favourite horse. But he must not reveal himself or else
he forfeits the rewards of patience and humility which
alone can make him attain his objective. This was the
warning of his Babalorisa, the priest of the Oracle. But
now a plague descends on humanity, for Oxala *is* the god
of creation. Rains cease, children die in their mothers'
wombs. In Ijimere's play:

> A curse has fallen on Oyo
> The corn on its stalk is worm-eaten
> And hollow like an old honeycomb;
> The yam in the earth is dry and
> Stringy like palm fibre...Creation comes to a
> standstill
> When he who turns blood into children
> Is lingering in jail. (*The Imprisonment of Obatala*, p. 31)

Complementarity is lost and balance is destroyed. Obatala (or Oxala) is the god who turns blood into children;
Ogun is the the god who turns children into blood. With
the former immobilised, Ogun comes into his own and
enjoys full ascendancy. There is distortion in the processes of the universe:

> The Bringer of Peace, the Father of Laughter
> Is locked in jail
> You have unleashed Ogun, who bathes in blood
> Even now does his reign begin.

He kills suddenly in the house and suddenly in the
field
He kills the child with iron with which it plays.
Ogun kills the slave-owner and the slaves as well
He kills the owner of the house and paints the
hearth with his blood! (p. 27)

It rains blood, earthquakes disrupt the city, beasts collapse and die in the forests, the rivers dry and the land
turns barren. In prison Obatala sits, instilling in all the
virtues of patience and fortitude, obedient to the injunc-
tions of the Ifa priest, Babalorisa. In Ijimere's version,
it is Esu who decides the nature of Obatala's punishment
and then torments him on the way. It is a trial of the spirit.

In both the Yoruba and the Brazilian versions, Obatala's journey is presented as a parable of confrontation
with Destiny. The initial motivation in Ijimere's play soon
becomes secondary: Obatala longs for the warm contact
of friendship. The new yam, he says, soft and creamy as
it is, has turned stringy in his mouth, the succulent meat
of the grass-cutter tastes gristly, and all because his friend
Sango is not there to share it with him. But even if this
craving were not present in Obatala, some other cause
would still have to be found, for the god of creation has
a date with Destiny at which his only weapon must be
patience. The Babalawo expounds his fortune and re-
minds him of his crime:

You drank the milky wine of the palm
Cool and sizzling it was in the morning,
Fermenting in the calabash
Its sweet foam overflowed
Like the eyes of a woman in love.
You refreshed yourself in the morning
But by evening time your hands were unsteady,
Your senses were dull, your fingertips numbed.
(p. 10)

He lists all the human deformities which resulted from Obatala's mortal slip and pronounces judgement: 'You must pay for your sins'.

Contrast this with the crime of the same deity in the Brazilian play. Yes, he does mould a deformed being but it is a deliberate act. Not only that, but the immediate victims of his aesthetic twist are not mortal beings but other deities – one a physical, the other a moral deformity. That this thereupon leads to a confrontation with Destiny is then attributed to the vanity and lack of understanding in a rather ill-tempered wife who would sooner have a son of external beauty than an ugly genius. Nowhere is Oxala held to have done wrong or committed any act that demands expiation. There results from this an abstract, disinterested quality about his sacrifice, one which suggests influences of the Christian passion play.

Sango's conduct in Ijimere's play compounds the criminality of the deities. Zora Zeljan ensures that in her version, Sango remains completely ignorant of the identity of the innocent sufferer. Not so in the Yoruba version. It is not merely the principle of justice which is abused in Sango's summary assumption of Obatala's guilt but, more eloquently, the demands of friendship and hospitality. Obatala's longing for the company of his fiery friend has been answered by a megalomaniac contempt:

> Is it possible that the wisest of all
> Should have become the most foolish?
> And the purest, the most foul?
> Oh horror, the father of laughter,
> Who rides the hunchback, has turned
> A common thief. (p. 22)

It is commonplace knowledge that hospitality is one of the most treasured laws of the African social existence. Sango's wife Oya is horrified by Sango's unthinking repudiation of friendship and seeks to assuage his anger by recalling to him Obatala's sumptuous reception of

Sango on a previous occasion; the praise-singing, the yam-pounding, the wine, the venison, the feasting. Sango places himself beyond reciprocation. With every plea, his hubris mounts. Every law of traditional social relationship is broken by the fiery god who is now beyond recall even to the demands of honourable or generous conduct. But the supreme act of hubris, the cosmic affront, lies in the fact that Obatala is the god of creation and may not be treated like an irrelevant factor in cosmic harmony. Oya is quick to remind her husband of the dangers of a disruption in the cosmic principle of complementarity, but Sango is beyond caring. Ogun now appears as the unchallenged half of the destructive–creative principle, for the destruction is not simply the physical havoc wreaked by Sango but a havoc done to Nature herself:

> Some women die in childbirth; they bleed
> Until their body is drained and dry.
> Or else the fruit rots in their womb
> Before it sees the light of day. (pp. 30–1)

'I fear', says Oya, who remains throughout the voice of reason and foresight, 'I fear that we are paying now for the king's injustice.'

Two gods, both guilty of anti-social behaviour. The consequences of their actions are experienced by their mortal subjects. The victims in Zora Zeljan's play are also mortals but both gods here are innocent of evil. Ironically, since we cannot but observe that the structural basis of Zora Zeljan's rites is the elicitation of 'essence', it should be remarked that it is in her version that Oxala is permitted a reduction of the 'pure stoic essence'. A beatific expression of godhead, yes; but although his physical sufferings appear to be greater than in *The Imprisonment,* he does not experience that level of rejection in Zeljan's play which he does in Ijimere's. Sango's rejection of him in Ijimere leaves Obatala with

22

no further recourse, no hope and no prospects of restitution. Moreover, since he is conscious of his own causa-
tive infraction, his situation must be one of guilt-laden
spiritual dejection. Oxala in the other play is constantly
reassured by knowledge of his complete innocence and
goodness and therefore of the certainty of vindication.
It is doubtful whether he could have reached the definitive level of rejection which fell to Obatala in *The
Imprisonment,* seeing that Obatala's primary objective
for that journey had deliberately made himself the
instrument of his humiliation. This, however, is by the
way. What Zeljan seems more concerned to establish is
the exact opposite of Ijimere – the conception of Sango
as a principle of Justice. And not Sango alone but all the
deities as principles, abstractions, essences. Transcendental emanations rather than flesh-and-blood creations.
Consider the following lines from *The Imprisonment*:

> So the new yam has come again
> Whiter than teeth, whiter than salt,
> Whiter than eyeballs,
> Whiter than the beads in my crown.
> Yam:
> You have the power to turn a wise man into a fool
> You cause the newly wedded wife to lose her
> manners
> The modest man unbuttons his shirt, his eyes grow
> wide
> The new yam knows no difference between beggar
> and king
> Between the thief and the rich man, between man
> and God;
> You turn them all greedy alike
> (*The Imprisonment of Obatala,* p. 3)

Or these, from Sango's verbal laceration of the hapless
Obatala:

> What madness to steal a horse he cannot ride

Like an impotent old chief
Who marries a moist young wife
And hides the shrivelled fruit
Between his legs.
Oh, had he tried to mount
This quivering black flame
He would have shook him off
Even quicker than the frustrated wife
Got rid of her limp husband
Who lacked the tool
To make her bleed and sweat. (pp. 24–5)

Such language will not be encountered in the Brazilian play. The Yoruba gods in the Brazilian version do not sweat or copulate. A scene such as takes place in Ijimere's play where Obatala not only argues with a clod of a farmer but is actually insulted and beaten to the ground by the mortal would be out of place in the Zeljan play. What we encounter in their place is the transcendentalist essence, the commencement of the attenuation of terrestrialism that I spoke of earlier, brought upon by the encounter of the gods with Christian saints.

Zeljan's kingdom of Sango is very much an Olympian setting. Even the boudoirs where the women of the gods meet, gossip and organise the day's domestic business is a bastion of divine remoteness. At the end of his ordeal, Oxala's reward to his wife for her faithfulness is a crown made of melted sun and precious stars. The effect of this aesthetic foundation is that even the ethical order and balances which are implicit in the play belong to a different order of existence, quite unlike the drama of Obatala where the pithiness of metaphor and the passions of the deities are brought to a terrestrial level, and the resolution – the moral elicited from the complementarity principle – is stated in terms of the well-being of the race. There is an allegorical distance about *The Feast of Bomfin*: the creatures who people it are unqestionably, and quite naturally, rarefied by the incorporeality of those saints with whom the Yoruba gods have become syncretised. Even in a forest setting:

> Iassan is happy and gay. She dances away with the light breezes from the woods! She dresses with gentle dry leaves and golden drops of morning dew! (*Oxala,* p. 22)

We will not find such ethereal imagery employed in the original homeland of these deities. Or again:

> What else do you want, exquisite one? Your face is as soft as dawn, your body moves with the elegance of sea waves. When you go to the spring for water the butterflies follow you and the trees bend down to touch you with their foliage. (p. 23)

In plays from the original source the gods are conceived more in the imagery of peat, chalk, oil, kernels, blood, heartwood and tuber, and active metaphors of human social preoccupations. (An incidental consideration is that in creating Omolu, Oxala stepped outside the elysian matrix of aesthetics and created a healer with the face of a yam tuber. A deplorable lapse into atavism perhaps, but hardly a sufficiently profound cause, were his wife Nana Buruku not culturally alienated, to generate a need in Nature for 'rites of passage'.) More seriously, however, the structural weakening of the dramatic moralities implicit in all such confrontations with Destiny is the logical result of this aesthetics of estrangement that defines, in the Brazilian play, the gods' reality. When ritual archetypes acquire new aesthetic characteristics, we may expect re-adjustments of the moral imperatives that brought them into existence in the first place, at the centre of man's efforts to order the universe.

There is far less of the essence of forbearance in the

composition of Ogun, the last of our three representative
deities. In an earlier essay of mine – 'The Fourth Stage'[7]
– I attempted to illustrate the essential Ogun using
Hellenic concepts as a combination of the Dionysian,
Apollonian and Promethean principles. In Yoruba metaphysics, no other deity in the pantheon correlates so
absolutely, through his own history and nature, with the
numinous temper of the fourth area of existence which
we have labelled the abyss of transition. Commonly
recognised in most African metaphysics are the three
worlds we have already discussed: the world of the
ancestor, the living and the unborn. Less understood or
explored is the fourth space, the dark continuum of
transition where occurs the inter-transmutation of
essence–ideal and materiality. It houses the ultimate expression of cosmic will.

Ogun's history is the story of the completion of Yoruba
cosmogony; he encapsulates that cosmogony's coming-
into-being in his own rites of passage. In our encounter
with Obatala we came across some rather sanguinary
lines which contrasted the nature of Ogun with that of
Obatala. So perhaps we ought to begin by redressing this
with other lines from Ogun's praise-chants, lines which
give a more balanced perspective of his truthful nature.
he is known as 'protector of orphans', 'roof over the
homeless', 'terrible guardian of the sacred oath'. He
stands for a transcendental, humane, but rigidly restorative justice:

> Rich-laden is his home, yet, decked in palm fronds
> He ventures forth, refuge of the down-trodden.
> To rescue slaves he unleashed the judgement of
> war
> Because of the blind, plunged into the forest
> Of curative herbs, Bountiful One

[7] In *The Morality of Art,* ed. D. W. Jefferson; reproduced here as
Appendix.

Who stands bulwark to offsprings of the dead in
heaven
Salutations O lone being, who bathes in rivers of
blood.

Yes, the blood is never completely absent, but at least we
know that this is not simply due to bloodthirstiness.

And Ogun is also the master craftsman and artist,
farmer and warrior, essence of destruction and creativity, a recluse and a gregarious imbiber, a reluctant
leader of men and deities. He is 'Lord of the road' of
Ifa; that is, he opens the way to the heart of Ifa's wisdom,
thus representing the knowledge-seeking instinct, an
attribute which sets him apart as the only deity who
'sought the way', and harnessed the resources of science
to hack a passage through primordial chaos for the gods'
reunion with man. The journey and its direction are at
the heart of Ogun's being and the relationship of the
gods and man. Its direction and motivation are also an
indication of the geocentric bias of the Yoruba, for it was
the gods who needed to come to man, anguished by a
continuing sense of incompleteness, needing to recover
their long-lost essence of totality. Ogun it was who led
them, his was the first rite of passage through the
chthonic realm.

The cause of the gods' spiritual unrest dated from their
own origin. Once, there was only the solitary being, the
primogenitor of god and man, attended only by his slave,
Atunda. We do not know where Atunda came from –
myth is always careless about detail – perhaps the original one moulded him from earth to assist him with
domestic chores. However, the slave rebelled. For reasons best known to himself he rolled a huge boulder on
to the god as he tended his garden on a hillside, sent him
hurtling into the abyss in a thousand and one fragments.
Again the figure varies. The fragmentation of the original godhead may be seen, however, as fundamental to

27

man's resolution of the experience of birth and the disintegration of consciousness in death. Ritualism itself is allied to these axial constants; in the gods' tragic drama the gods serve as media for this central experience, the conflicts and events are active contrivances for ease of entry into the experience, dramatic motifs whose aesthetic formalism dissolves the barrier of individual distance.

The creation of the multiple godhead began a transference of social functions, the division of labour and professions among the deities whose departments they were thereafter to become. The shard of original Oneness which contained the creative flint appears to have passed into the being of Ogun, who manifests a temperament for artistic creativity matched by technological proficiency. His world is the world of craft, song and poetry. The practitioners of *Ijala,* the supreme lyrical form of Yoruba poetic art, are followers of Ogun the hunter. Ijala celebrates not only the deity but animal and plant life, seeks to capture the essence and relationships of growing things and the insights of man into the secrets of the universe. With creativity, however, went its complementary aspect, and Ogun came to symbolise the creative–destructive principle. This does not in any way usurp the province of Obatala whose task is to create the lifeless form of man. Nor is Obatala ever moved to destroy. Obatala is a functionalist of creation, not, like Ogun, the essence of creativity itself.

Yet none of them, not even Ogun, was complete in himself. There had to be a journey across the void to drink at the fount of mortality though, some myths suggest, it was really to inspect humanity and see if the world peopled by the mortal shards from the common ancestor was indeed thriving. But the void had become impenetrable. A long isolation from the world of men had created an impassable barrier which they tried, but failed, to demolish. Ogun finally took over. Armed with the first technical instrument which he had forged from the ore of mountain-wombs, he cleared the primordial jungle, plunged through the abyss and called on the others to follow. For this feat the gods offered him a crown, inviting him to be king over them. Ogun refused. Human society was to commit the same error, and to prove sufficiently persistent to sway him from his wisely considered refusal. On arrival on earth, the various deities went their way, observing and inspecting. Ogun in his wanderings came to the town of Ire where he was well received, later returning its hospitality when he came to its aid against an enemy. In gratitude he was offered the crown of Ire. He declined and retired into the mountains where he lived in solitude, hunting and farming. Again and again he was importuned by the elders of Ire until he finally consented.

When he first descended among them, the people took to their heels. Ogun presented a face of himself which he hoped would put an end to their persistence. He came down in his leather war-kit, smeared in blood from head to foot. When they had fled he returned to his mountain-lair, satisfied that the lesson had been implanted. Alas, back they came again. They implored him, if he would only come in less terrifying attire, they would welcome him as king and leader. Ogun finally consented. He came down decked in palm fronds and was crowned king. In war after war he led his men to victory. Then, finally, came the day when, during a lull in the battle, our old friend Esu the trickster god left a gourd of palm wine for the thirsty deity. Ogun found it exceptionally delicious and drained the gourd to the dregs. In that battle the enemy was routed even faster than usual, the carnage was greater than ever before. But by now, to the drunken god, friend and foe had become confused; he turned on his men and slaughtered them. This was the possibility that had haunted him from the beginning and made him shrink from the role of king over men. Such, however, is the wilful nature of Ogun that he does not, unlike Obatala, forbid the use of palm wine in his worship – on the contrary. Ogun is the embodiment of challenge, the Promethean instinct in man, constantly at the service of society for its full self-realisation. Hence his role of explorer through primordial chaos, which he conquered, then bridged, with the aid of the artifacts of his science. The other deities following through the realm of transition could only share vicariously in the original experience. Only Ogun experienced the process of being literally torn asunder in cosmic winds, of rescuing himself from the precarious edge of total dissolution by harnessing the untouched part of himself, the will, This is the unique essentiality of Ogun in Yoruba metaphysics: as embodiment of the social, communal will invested in a protagonist of its choice. It is as a paradigm of this experience of dissolution and re-integration that the actor in the ritual of archetypes can be understood.

Ogun's action did not take place in a vacuum. His venture was, necessarily a drama of individual stress, yet even his moment of individuation was communicant, one which enabled the other gods to share, whose end-in-view was no less than a strengthening of the communal psyche. This is a different dimension from Obatala's internalised saintly passage or Sango's destructive egotism. The action has been undertaken both on the practical and on the symbolic level of protagonist for the community. The actor in ritual drama operates in the same way. He prepares mentally and physically for his disintegration and re-assembly within the universal womb of origin, experiences the transitional yet inchoate matrix of death and being. Such an actor in the role of the protagonist becomes the unresisting mouthpiece of the god, uttering sounds which he barely comprehends but which are reflections of the awesome glimpse of that transitional gulf, the seething cauldron of the dark world-will and psyche. Tragic feeling in Yoruba drama stems from sympathetic knowledge of the protagonist's foray into this psychic abyss of the re-creative energies.

It is because of the reality of this gulf, this abyss, so crucial to Yoruba cosmic ordering, that Ogun becomes a key figure in understanding the Yoruba metaphysical world. The gulf is what must constantly be diminished (or rendered less threateningly remote) by sacrifices, rituals, ceremonies of appeasement to the cosmic powers which lie guardian to the gulf. Ogun, by incorporating within himself so many seemingly contradictory attributes, represents the closest conception to the original oneness of Orisa-nla. Significantly, his festival is climaxed by the symbolic sacrifice of his favourite animal. A dog, now a surrogate for the god, is cut clean through the neck. After this, a symbolic mock-struggle takes place between the priest and his acolytes for the possession of the body, that is, the god. Earlier, the staff of Ogun, represented by long willowy poles topped by lumps of ore bound in palm frond, is borne by men through the town. The heavy ore at the top and the suppleness of the wood strain the stave in vibrant curves, forcing the men to move about among the revellers who constantly yield them room as they seek to keep the pole balanced. They then go up to the grove of Ogun in the mountain-tops where more revellers are decked in palm fronds and bear palm branches in their hands.

The dynamic fusion in the wilful nature of Ogun, represented in the dance of lumps of ore, is complemented by the peaceful symbolism of the palm in which the ore is bound; the men's manic leaps up the hillside by the beatific recessional of the women who meet them at the foothills and accompany them home with song. Through it all – in the association of the palm frond with the wine of Ogun's error, yet the symbol of his peaceful nature; the aggressive ore and its restraining fronds, a balletic tension of balance in the men with the leaded poles; in the fusion of image and fertility invocations in the straining phallus-heads framed against the sky and the thudding feet of sweat-covered men on the earth; in the resonant rhythms of Ogun's iron gongs and the peaceful resolution of the indigo figures and voices of women on the plain – a dynamic marriage unfolds of the aesthetics of ritualism and the moralities of control, balance, sacrifice, the protagonist spirit and the imperatives of cohesion, diffusing a spiritual tonality that enriches the individual being and the community.

George Thomson in his *Aeschylus and Athens* (Lawrence & Wishart, 1941) comes very close to giving a perceptive description of the process by which the office of the protagonist actor transcends the actual conflict of the ritual and conveys the deeper experience of a challenger of the transitional abyss. But he shies away finally from the fullness of his obvious illumination, and retracts in mid-word the observable reality of the protagonist–audience relation. This is an interesting example of what results when scholars subvert their intelligent deductions to imperatives of alien and jealous gods, in his case, Marxism:

> Myth was created out of ritual. The latter term
> must be understood in a wide sense, because in
> primitive society everything is sacred, nothing
> profane. Every action – eating, drinking, tilling,
> fighting – has its proper procedure, which being
> prescribed, is holy. (pp. 63–4)

This, of course, is what Jonathan Swift would call 'enthusiasm', a pardonable exaggeration common to the more positive among foreign sociologists. Herskovits was another notable sinner in this respect in his efforts to understand traditional African theatre. However, Thomson continues:

> In the song and dance of the mimetic rite, each
> performer withdrew, under the hypnotic effect of

rhythm, from the consciousness of reality, which
was peculiar to himself, individual, into the
subconscious world of fantasy, which was common
to all, collective, and from that inner world they
returned *charged with new strength for action.*
Poetry and dancing, which grew out of the mimetic
rite, are speech and gesture raised to a magical level
of intensity. For a long time, in virtue of their
common origin and function, they were inseparable.
The divergence of poetry from dancing, of myth
from ritual, only began with the rise of the ruling
class whose culture was divorced from the labour of
production. (p. 64)

We shall leave the latter Marxist speculations alone, as
being outside the scope of this subject. The points which
concern us here are (1) the recognition of the integral
nature of poetry and dancing in the mimetic rite, and
(2) the withdrawal of the individual into an inner world
from which he returns, communicating a new strength
for action. The definition of this inner world as 'fantasy'
betrays a Eurocentric conditioning or alienation. We
describe it as the primal reality, the hinterland of transition. The community emerges from ritual experience
'charged with new strength for action' because of the
protagonist's Promethean raid on the durable resources
of the transitional realm; immersed within it, he is enab-
led empathically to transmit its essence to the choric
participants of the rites – the community. Nor would we
consider that such a communicant withdraws from conscious reality, but rather that his consciousness is stretched
to embrace another and primal reality. The communicant effect on the audience which is the choric vessel and
earthing mechanism for the venturer is not a regression
into 'the subconscious world of fantasy'. Except through
mass hypnotism, which is not suggested by Thomson,
fantasy is individual and incommunicable – at least, not

until after the event, and only by graphic or verbal means. To describe a *collective* inner world as fantasy is not intelligible, for the nature of an inner world in a cohesive society is the essentialisation of a rational world-view, one which is elicited from the reality of social and natural experience and from the integrated reality of racial myths into a living morality. The electronic (or is it simply telepathic?) transmission of ideograms of a collective fantasy is a fantasy of its claimants only. What is transmitted in ritual is essence and response, the residual energies from the protagonist's excursion into the realm of cosmic will which, in Thomson's expressive phrase, charges the community with new strength for action.

But perhaps Thomson's understanding derives from Jung's theories. Jung, begetter of so many racist distortions of the structure of the human psyche, interchangably employs ritual archetypes and images of psychotic fantasy. While the intrusion of archetypal images into the psychotic condition (or fevered, drunken deliriums for that matter) is an acknowledged occurrence, Jung's perception becomes narrowed in his indifferently hierarchic relation of such products of the disturbed mind to the immanent quality of the ritual archetype. The one is a de-contextualised, unharmonised homologue (at best!) of the other, deprived of meaning and relatedness (or wrenched out of normal relations into abnormal ones). Image shorn of, cut off from, symbolic relations with apprehended reality. The profession of the psycho-analyst lies in the sorting out of the new discrete images from their hostile environment; he has no equipment (as an outsider) for the equation of such images themselves with the essence–reality of their origin. Where illusion besets the analyst is when new patterns of discrete components, because they attain a consistent direction of their own, are taken to simulate or reflect the cohesive archetypal motifs of a primal inner world.

'Primitive mentality' declared Jung (and his assumptions are based on *living* examples, not on a retrospective projection into human development), 'differs from civilized chiefly in that the conscious mind is far less developed in extent and intensity. Functions such as thinking, willing etc. are not yet differentiated...[the primitive] is incapable of any conscious effort of will... owing to the chronic twilight state of his conscious, it is often next to impossible to find out whether he merely dreamed something or whether he really experienced it ...'.[8] And so, on the authority of European ethnologists who lack the *language* to penetrate the Australian and other natives' own significations of 'dreaming', 'experiencing', 'thinking' and so on, Jung proceeds to identify the territories of dream, fantasy, psychotic exhalations etc., with the historic–empirical–ethical–psychic structure in which the ritual archetype is housed. What *we* call the mythic inner world is both the psychic sub-structure and temporal subsidence, the cumulative history and empirical observations of the community. It is nonetheless primal in that time, in its cyclic reality, is fundamental to it. The inner world is not static, being constantly enriched by the moral and historic experience of man. Jung, by contrast declares that 'the archetype does not proceed from physical facts'. So it is primordially autogenous? The contradictions suggested by other observations, such as 'the archetype...mediates between the unconscious substratum and the conscious mind...', 'throws a bridge between the consciousness of the present...and the natural, unconscious, instinctive wholeness of primeval times' is explainable by this simple observation: that Jung differentiates the nature of the archetype in the 'primitive' mind from that of the 'civilised' mind even as he pays lip-service to the universality of a collective unconscious, and to the archetype as the inhabitant of that hinterland.

[8] Jung and Kerenyi, *Introduction to a Science of Mythology*, p. 101.

The means to our inner world of transition, the vortex of archetypes and kiln of primal images is the ritualised experience of the gods themselves and of Ogun most especially. Nor is Ogun's identification with the innate mythopoeia of music fortuitous. Music is the intensive language of transition and its communicant means, the catalyst and solvent of its regenerative hoard. The actor dares not venture into this world unprepared, without symbolic sacrifices and the invocation of eudaemonic guardians of the abyss. In the symbolic disintegration and retrieval of the protagonist ego is reflected the destiny of being. This is ritual's legacy to later tragic art, that the tragic hero stands to his contemporary reality as the ritual protagonist on the edge of transitional gulf; alas, the evolution of tragic art in the direction of the specific event has shrunk its cosmic scope, however closely the hero approaches the archetypal. And its morality has become a mere extraction of the intellect, separated from the total processes of being and human continuity.

2

Drama and the African world-view

First, let us dispose of some red herrings. The serious divergences between a traditional African approach to drama and the European will not be found in lines of opposition between creative individualism and communal creativity, nor in the level of noise from the auditorium – this being the supposed gauge of audience-participation – at any given performance. They will be found more accurately in what is a recognisable Western cast of mind, a compartmentalising habit of thought which periodically selects aspects of human emotion, phenomenal observations, metaphysical intuitions and even scientific deductions and turns them into separatist myths (or 'truths') sustained by a proliferating super-structure of presentation idioms, analogies and analytical modes. I have evolved a rather elaborate metaphor to describe it; appropriately it is not only mechanistic but represents a period technology which marked yet another phase of Western man's comprehensive world-view.

You must picture a steam-engine which shunts itself between rather closely-spaced suburban stations. At the first station it picks up a ballast of allegory, puffs into the next emitting a smokescreen on the eternal landscape of nature truths. At the next it loads up with a different species of logs which we shall call naturalist timber, puffs into a half-way stop where it fills up with the synthetic fuel of surrealism, from which point yet another holistic world-view is glimpsed and asserted through psychedelic smoke. A new consignment of absurdist coke lures it into the next station from which it departs giving off no smoke at all, and no fire, until it derails briefly along constructivist tracks and is towed back to the starting-point by a neo-classic engine.

This, for us, is the occidental creative rhythm, a series of intellectual spasms which, especially today, appears susceptible even to commercial manipulation. And the difference which we are seeking to define between European and African drama as one of man's formal representation of experience is not simply a difference of style or form, nor is it confined to drama alone. It is representative of the essential differences between two world-views, a difference between one culture whose very artifacts are evidence of a cohesive understanding of irreducible truths and another, whose creative impulses are directed by period dialectics. So, to begin with, we must jettison that fashionable distinction which tends to encapsulate Western drama as a form of esoteric enterprise spied upon by fee-paying strangers, as contrasted with a communal evolution of the dramatic mode of expression, this latter being the African. Of far greater importance is the fact that Western dramatic criticism habitually reflects the abandonment of a belief in culture as defined within man's knowledge of fundamental, unchanging relationships between himself and society and within the larger context of the observable universe.

Let us, by way of a paradigmatic example, take a common theme in traditional mask-drama: a symbolic struggle with chthonic presences, the goal of the conflict being a harmonious resolution for plenitude and the well-being of the community.[1] Any individual within the 'audience' knows better than to add his voice *arbitrarily* even to the most seductive passages of an invocatory song, or to contribute a refrain to the familiar sequence

[1] The remarks which follow are based on plays observed *in situ*, that is, on the spot where the performance originates and ends, and at its appropriate time of the year, not itinerant variations on the same theme. The specific play referred to here was a harvest play which took place on a farm-clearing some three miles south of Ihiala in the then Eastern Region of Nigeria, 1961.

of liturgical exchanges among the protagonists. The moment for choric participation is well-defined, but this does not imply that until such a moment, participation ceases. The so-called audience is itself an integral part of that arena of conflict; it contributes spiritual strength to the protagonist through its choric reality which must first be conjured up and established, defining and investing the arena through offerings and incantations. The drama would be non-existent except within and against this symbolic representation of earth and cosmos, except within this communal compact whose choric essence supplies the collective energy for the challenger of chthonic realms. Overt participation when it comes is channelled through a formalised repertoire of gestures and liturgical responses. The 'spontaneous' participant from within the audience does not permit himself to give vent to a bare impulse or a euphoria which might bring him out as a dissociated entity from within the choric mass. If it does happen, as of course it can, the event is an aberration which may imperil the eudaemonic goals of that representation. The interjector – whose balance of mind is regarded as being temporarily disturbed – is quietly led out and the appropriate (usually unobtrusive) spells are cast to counter the risks of the abnormal event.

I would like to go a little deeper into this ritualistic sense of space since it is so intimately linked with the comprehensive world-view of the society that gave it birth. We shall treat it first as a medium in the communicative sense and, like any other medium, it is one that is best defined through the process of interruption. In theatrical terms, this interruption is effected principally by the human apparatus. Sound, light, motion, even smell, can all be used just as validly to define space, and ritual theatre uses all these instruments of definition to control and render concrete, to parallel (this is perhaps the best description of the process) the experiences or intuitions of man in that far more disturbing environment which he defines variously as void, emptiness or infinity. The concern of ritual theatre in this process of spatial definition which precedes, as we shall discover, the actual enactment must therefore be seen as an integral part of man's constant efforts to master the immensity of the cosmos with his minuscule self. The actual events which make up the enactment are themselves, in ritual theatre, a materialisation of this basic adventure of man's metaphysical self.

Theatre then is one arena, one of the earliest that we know of, in which man has attempted to come to terms with the spatial phenomenon of his being. Again, in speaking of space, let us recognise first of all that with the advancement of technology and the evolution – some would prefer to call it a counter-evolution – of the technical sensibility, the spatial vision of theatre has become steadily contracted into purely physical acting areas on a stage as opposed to a symbolic arena for metaphysical contests. The pagan beginnings of Greek theatre retained their symbolic validity to dramaturgists for centuries after the event, so that the relative positions of suppliant, tyrant or *deus ex machina,* as well as the offertory or altar, were constantly impressed on their audience and created immediate emotional overtones both when they were used and by their very act of being. (I do not, for the purpose of this essay, wish to debate whether the fixity of these positions did not, contrasted with the fluid approach of African ritual space, detract from the audience's experience of cosmic relations.) Medieval European theatre in its turn, corresponding to the religious mythology of its period, created a constant *microcosmos* by its spatial correspondences of good and evil, angels and demons, paradise, purgatory and hell. The protagonists of earth, heaven and hell enacted their various trials and conflicts in relation to these traditional positions, and the automatic recognition of these hierarchical situations of man created spiritual anxieties and hopes in the breasts of the audience. But observe, the apprehended territory of man has already begun to contract! Cosmic representation has shrunk into a purely moral one, a summation in terms of penalties and rewards. The process continued through successive periods of European partial explorations of what was once a medium of totality, achieving such analytical aberrations as in this sample of compartmentalisation which claims that the right (actor's) wing of the stage is 'stronger' than the left. We shall not encounter any proofs of this ludicrous assertion in the beginnings of theatre, Greek or African.

Ritual theatre, let it be recalled, establishes the spatial medium not merely as a physical area for simulated events but as a manageable contraction of the cosmic envelope within which man – no matter how deeply buried such a consciousness has latterly become – fearfully exists. And this attempt to manage the immensity of his spatial awareness makes every manifestation in ritual theatre a paradigm for the cosmic human condition. There are transient parallels, brief visual moments of this experience in modern European theatre. The spectacle of a lone human figure under a spotlight on a darkened stage is, unlike a painting, a breathing, living, pulsating, threateningly fragile example of this paradigm. It is threatening because, unlike a similar parable on canvas, its fragility is experienced both at the level of its symbolism and in terms of sympathetic concern for the well-being of that immediate human medium. Let us say he is a tragic character: at the first sign of a check in the momentum of a tragic declamation, his audience becomes nervous for him, wondering – has he forgotten his line? has he blacked out? Or in the case of opera – will she make that upper register? Well, ritual theatre has an additional, far more fundamental anxiety. Indeed, it is correct to say that the technical anxiety even where it exists – after all it does

exist; the element of creative form is never absent even
in the most so-called primitive consciousness – so, where
it does exist, it is never so profoundly engaged as with
a modern manifestation. The real unvoiced fear is: will
this protagonist survive confrontation with forces that
exist within the dangerous area of transformation? En-
tering that *microcosmos* involves a loss of individuation,
a self-submergence in universal essence. It is an act
undertaken on behalf of the community, and the welfare
of that protagonist is inseparable from that of the total
community.[2]

This ritual understanding is essential to a profound
participation in the cathartic processes of the great
tragedies. To attempt to define it even more clearly I
would like to refer once again to painting, that essentially
individualistic art. In surmounting the challenge of space
and cosmos, a Turner, a Wyeth or a van Gogh utilises
endless permutations of colour, shapes and lines to
extract truly harrowing or consoling metaphysical statements from natural phenomena. There is, however, no
engagement of the communal experience in this particular medium. The transmission is individual. It is no less
essential to the sum of human experience but it is, even
when viewed by a thousand people simultaneously, a
mere sum of fragmented experiences, individual and
vicarious. The singularity of theatre is its simultaneity in
the forging of a single human experience – at its most
successful. That it does not often succeed is true enough,
but that does not invalidate the truth that, at the very
roots of the dramatic phenomenon, this affirmation of
the communal self was the experiential goal The search,
even by modern European dramatists for ritualist roots
from which to draw out visions of modern experience,
is a clue to the deep-seated need of creative man to

[2] Kola Ogunmola, in his stage adaptations of Amos Tutuola's
Palmwine Drinkard built on this tradition, one that is still manifested
in ancestral mask comedies.

recover this archetypal consciousness in the origins of the dramatic medium.

Ritual theatre, viewed from the spatial perspective, aims to reflect through physical and symbolic means the archetypal struggle of the mortal being against exterior forces. A tragic view of the theatre goes further and suggests that even the so-called realistic or literary drama can be interpreted as a mundane reflection of this essential struggle. Poetic drama especially may be regarded as a repository of this essential aspect of theatre; being largely metaphorical, it expands the immediate meaning and action of the protagonists into a world of nature forces and metaphysical conceptions. Or, to put it the other way round, powerful natural or cosmic influences are internalised within the protagonists and this implosive factor creates the titanic scale of their passions even when the basis of the conflict seems hardly to warrant it. (Shakespeare's *Lear* is the greatest exemplar of this.) Indeed, this view of theatre sees the stage as a constant battleground for forces larger than the petty infractions of habitual communal norms or patterns of human relationships and expectations, beyond the actual twists and incidents of action and their resolutions. The stage is created for the purpose of that communal presence which alone defines it (and this is the fundamental defining concept, that the stage is brought into being by a communal presence); so, for this purpose, the stage becomes the affective, rational and intuitive milieu of the total communal experience, historic, race-formative, cosmogonic. Where such theatre is encountered in its purest form, not as re-created metaphors for the later tragic stage, we will find no compass points, no horizontal or vertical definitions. There are no reserved spaces for the protagonists, for his very act of representational being is defined in turn by nothing less than the infinite cosmos within which the origin of the community and its contemporaneous experience of being is firmly embedded.

Drama, however, exists on the boards; in the improvised space among stalls in the deserted or teeming market, on the raised platform in a school or community hall, in the secretive recesses of a nature-fringed shrine, among the push-buttons of the modern European stage or its equivalents in Africa – those elegant monstrosities raised to enshrine the spirit of misconceived prestigiousness. It is necessary always to look for the essence of the play among these roofs and spaces, not confine it to the printed text as an autonomous entity. For this reason, deductions from plays which have had the benefit of actual production are more instructive and, for the rest of this chapter, I intend to utilise two different but representative plays which have had the benefit of realisation before both European and African audiences. Critical responses are in themselves an index of dramatic attitudes and are, even more relevantly, a reflection of those world-views which separate and profoundly affect the relations of art and life in differing cultures. A ground common to all fortunately makes comparative references possible: the creative man is universally involved in a subtle conspiracy, a tacit understanding that he, the uncommissioned observer, relates the plight of man, his disasters and joys, to some vague framework of observable truths and realities. The differences in attitudes will be found in the categories given to realities which are common to all, the relative comprehensiveness of vision, and the assumptions which the creative mind feels traditionally entitled to make or turn into acceptances – from the forcefulness of his art – coerced from the most unwilling audience.

Our first example, *Song of a Goat,* a play by J. P. Clark,[2] has the advantage, for this exercise, of fitting into the neat category of tragedy in the European definition. It was first performed in Europe at the 1965 Common-

[3] In J. P. Clark, *Three Plays,* Oxford University Press, 1964.

wealth Festival of the Arts in London; its reception was not of the best, and for very good reasons. Firstly, the production was weak and amateurish. An inexperienced group playing on a London stage for the first time in their lives found that they could not match the emotions of the play with the technical demands of the stage and auditorium. The staging of the play was not particularly sensitive, in addition to which there were the usual unscripted happenings which seem to plague amateur productions everywhere. A rather lively goat, another practical mistake, tended to punctuate passages of intended solemnity with bleats from one end and something else from the other. The text itself (we may as well get over the critical carps at once), written in verse, betrays a self-conscious straining for poetic effect, leading to inflated phrasing and clotted passages. For a company which was not wholly at home in the English language, the difficulties were insurmountable. In an English audience it created resistance, even hostility.

The drama takes place in a fishing village. The characters are Ijaw, a riverine people on the Niger delta. Two brothers, Zifa and Tonye, Ebiere the wife of Zifa the elder brother, and Orukorere, a scatty old aunt of the two brothers, are the central characters. The old lady provides a Cassandra-presence throughout the unfolding of the tragedy which is centred on the sexual impotence of Zifa.

At first Zifa sends his wife to consult the Masseur, a doctor-cum-seer who diagnoses the real problem without difficulty, recognises that it is the husband not the wife who is the real patient. He suggests that the younger brother, Tonye, take up the marital duties of the elder, an idea which is violently rejected by Zifa (who later consults him) just as Ebiere indignantly spurns it in her turn. But the inevitable does happen. In one of the most credible scenes of progressive sexual frustration Ebiere goads the brother into taking her. Zifa suspects,

45

manoeuvres the guilty pair into a revelatory ritual – this ritual is made the climactic moment of the play – and tries to kill Tonye. He escapes, only to hang himself in the loft. Zifa walks out to sea and the house of Zifa is left to the bats and goats.

I have touched on some of the technical reasons why, unlike some African audiences before whom this play has since been staged, the European audience found itself estranged from the tragic statement. One other reason was voiced by the newspaper critics; this had nothing to do with the fortuitous events of stage presentation but rather chose to limit, in far more general terms, what areas of human unhappiness may contain the tragic potential. It underlined yet another aspect of the essential divergences of the European cast of mind from the African: that, on the one hand, which sees the cause of human anguish as viable only within strictly temporal capsules, and the other, whose tragic understanding transcends the causes of individual disjunction and recognises them as reflections of a far greater disharmony in the communal psyche. The objection was this: sexual impotence was a curable condition in modern medicine (or psychiatry). In addition, child adoption provided one remedy, among others, for sterility; therefore sexual impotence or sterility were outside the range of tragic dimensions for a European audience.

There was something familiar in that plaint. I had heard it some years earlier after a London production of Ibsen's *Ghosts*. Syphilis, asserted a critic or two, was no longer an incurable disease. Ibsen's play had consequently lost any tragic rationale it might have had in the mercury days of venereal science. I could not help recalling this particular critical thesis when I found myself in Sydney a year or two after this and encountered an Australian poet who, with his wife cheerfully supplying details, boasted that he had caught a completely new mutation of the syphilitic virus which had the entire

Australian medical profession stumped. Nicknamed the Golden Staphylococcus because of its appearance under the microscope, it had developed powerful resistance to all known antibiotics. Research and consultations with international laboratories would shortly, I was relieved to learn, put an end to the reign of the Golden Staphylococcus, but I could not help wondering aloud if Ibsen's *Ghosts* should not quickly be declared the definitive antipodean tragedy of the sixties.

Our critic would have found consolation, however, even confirmation of his views, in the quiet cheerful attitude towards the acquisition of a new and rather menacing bacillus. He would fall back on the argument that the social atmosphere created by the demystification of diseases, and the removal of the puritanical burden of opprobrium which attached to the 'social' diseases have combined to destroy the genetic doom which gave Ibsen's tragedy its dimension of the inescapable. Thus too O'Neill and his tuberculosis-infested drama. And so attitudes which consider sexual impotence as insufficient cause for a statement in tragic terms are logical results of sociological changes, a relaxation of traditional attitudes to masculine virility, and the existence of opportunities through which the creative constriction in the victim can be channelled. Indeed, to sum it up in the most contemporary terms, Women's Lib. and the tragedy of sexual impotence, or even infidelity, are mutually exclusive. *The Father* is dead; long live *The Female Eunuch*!

The socio-political question of the viability of a tragic view in a contemporary world has preoccupied schools of social vision since the preliminary clashes of the empirical stance against metaphysical (religious) orthodoxies. This has become crystallised in, I suggest, two main attitudes. One, represented by the Marxist view of man and history, denounces the insidious enervation of social will by the tragic afflatus. The other is the rear-guard action of crumbling defences. It speculates that there has been a decline in tragic understanding (i.e. the referential basis from which man is convincingly projected in confrontation with forces beyond his remedial understanding). From this basis of suspicion and a related awareness that this represents a quite unnecessary loss in creative territory, an almost comprehensive list of major twentieth century dramatists have felt compelled, at one time or the other, to rifle and re-present Greek tragedy as containing statements of relevance even to post-Marxian times.

Among the literary beneficiaries of the first attitude, the principle of a revolutionary rejection of the ineffable, is the French neo-fiction movement of the late fifties and early sixties (Robbe-Grillet etc.) whose manifesto enjoins the fictional realisation (observe the contradiction) of objective superficies. Rooted in as deep a fallacy as the involuted Surrealist ontology which it appears to oppose, the theory of the new fiction both creates a gulf between man and his physical environment and declares the gulf unbridgeable. What we are confronted with in these seemingly antagonistic views are two faces of the same European tradition: one which assumes and seeks to transcend a gulf between man and the essence of being, thought, feeling etc., between object and the pure state of being; and the other which, claiming to rectify the anti-social pursuit of an intangible kingdom by this and other schools of world-perception, legislates a gulf between man and the materiality of his environment and proceeds to employ consciously mechanistic devices to widen the unproven, purely hypothetical abyss.

George Steiner observes, in his diagnosis of the decline in tragic grandeur of the European dramatic vision,[4] a relatedness between this decline and that of the 'organic world view and of its attendant context of mythological, symbolic and ritual reference'. The implication of this,

[4] George Steiner, *The Death of Tragedy,* Faber, London, 1963; see chapters 6 and 9.

a strange one to the African world-view, is that, to expand Steiner's own metaphor, the world in which lightning was a cornice in the cosmic architecture of man collapsed at that moment when Benjamin Franklin tapped its power with a kite. The assimilative wisdom of African metaphysics recognises no difference in essence between the mere means of tapping the power of lightning – whether it is by ritual sacrifice, through the purgative will of the community unleashing its justice on the criminal, or through the agency of Franklin's revolutionary gadget. What George Steiner effectively summarises is that at some stage of intellectual hypothesis, at some phase of scientific exploration, at each supposition by European man about the possible nature of things, that architectonic unity which is the basis of man's regulating consciousness (of which the most personalised expression is his art) suffers the same fate of redundancy as the assumptions and theories themselves. For cultures which pay more than lip-service to the protean complexity of the universe of which man is himself a reflection, this European habit of world re-definition appears both wasteful and truth-defeating.

We must return to the stage manifestation, to the dramatic expression which confronts its audience with such human revelations as breed an awareness of a play of forces which contradict a technologically remediable world, this being the most easily isolated challenge of the tragic intrusion. It becomes necessary to examine the nature of the concrete event which, when successfully mirrored, dislodges the technological rationale with which the healthy, well-adjusted audience is conditioned to ward off penetration of the 'pathetic fallacy'.

And the most significant discovery, or more accurately, recognition is that we encounter in such plays a complete, hermetic universe of forces or being. This is the most fundamental attribute of all true tragedy, no matter where geographically placed. In *Lear* for instance, the world of the court, the world of Old Man Frost in the disordered community of wind and heather is rounded and entire. The relationship of seemingly disparate entities such as Court and Nature is established through character transition – Lear, Kent, Edgar and Clown, out from one and into the other environment and back again; then the progressively vixenish daughters in near physical transformation. Such is the spatial architecture of the play that the specialised world of cronies, villains, principles of inheritance and courtly protocol becomes accessible to and paralleled by whatever world the audience inhabits, with its own laws, norms and values. The universe of *Hamlet* is wrapped in a similar envelope; so are the haunting habitations of John Synge, Garcia Lorca, even Wedekind at his most uncompromising interiority. Encapsulation of these exclusivist spheres of existence within which all action is unravelled appears to be the first prerequisite of all profound drama, and tragedy most specifically. Its internal cogency makes it impervious to the accident of place and time.

In relating *Song of a Goat* to such drama, I make no exaggerated claims for its actual achievement. It remains, however, an excellent premise from which to enter the matrical consciousness of the African world. The play is contained within a microcosmic completeness as already described, with especially strong affinities – again for ease of reference – to the world of Lorca. A play of brooding violence, its central motif, the symbolic design, may be described as one of contained, poetic violence. We encounter human beings whose occupation and environment are elemental and visceral. Flood and ebb affect their daily existence, their language, their spectrum of perception. Mists and marsh colour their mood. Within this claustrophobia of threatening metaphors, existence is economical and intense; its expansion into an awareness of immediately exterior forces merely reinforces their circumscribed intensity of being. From this closed relationship a thread of potential violence is gradually drawn, consistently prepared through metaphors within the dialogue of action. Until we are brought at last, bound to the protagonists, to the climactic image which, for the principal sufferer, is also the image of revelation – a sacrificial pot and the ram's head within it, a precariously contained force, barely held, barely restrained. It parallels that core of sexual frustration, that damming up of natural continuity and beneficient release by sterile opposition compounded with individual pride, self-deception, a code of morality which presupposes normal circumstances. The whole point, however, is that the circumstances are abnormal, even unnatural. The interaction of man and nature so pervasively rendered in the play demands a drastic redress of these abnormal circumstances, and it is a demand which cannot be pushed aside by the pride of one man. The poetic containment of violence is very much the environmental reality of *Song of a Goat*. Storms do not occur every day nor are fishermen washed off their canoes on every fishing-trip. But the hovering claims of this natural cycle dominate the natives' daily awareness, giving to rituals of appeasement an integrated essentiality for every event. Thus the death of an individual is not seen as an isolated incident in the life of one man. Nor is individual fertility separable from the regenerative promise of earth and sea. The sickness of one individual is a sign of, or may portend the sickness of, the world around him. Something has occurred to disrupt the natural rhythms and the cosmic balances of the total community.

> There, another blow
> Has been dealt the tree of our house, and see
> How the sap pours out to spread our death. I
> Believe it, now I believe it. White ants
> Have passed their dung on our roof-top.
> Like a tree rotten in the rain, it

51

Topples. What totem is there left now
For the tribe to hold on to for support! (p. 42)

Passages like this, displaying few of the lapses of language
which mar a good portion of the play, convey an
unselfconscious conjunction of the circumcentric worlds
of man, social community and Nature in the minds of
each character, irrespective of role. And one important,
even vital, element in the composition of the elaborate
interiority of such a world is, of course, its moral order.
This must not be understood in any narrow sense of the
ethical code which society develops to regulate the conduct of its members. A breakdown in moral order
implies, in the African world-view, a rupture in the body
of Nature just like the physical malfunctioning of one
man. And the literature of this viewpoint is not to be
found in the ruminative asides or debates among princi-
pals but in the metaphor of existence in the most mundane or in the most exalted circumstances. We find, to
revert to J. P. Clark's play, that moral disorder is not
simply a matter of sleeping with another man's wife,
especially if that man is your brother. This is of course
an anti-social act and it is recognised as such. It is neither
desirable nor is it condoned. Deviations from harmonious conduct such as this are dealt with by set
processes which vary from society to society. But this
anti-social act can be, depending on circumstances, a far
less dangerous threat to communal well-being than, for
instance, Zifa's self-delusion and sterile pride.

Where society lives in a close inter-relation with
Nature, regulates its existence by natural phenomena
within the observable processes of continuity – ebb and
tide, waxing and waning of the moon, rain and drought,
planting and harvest – the highest moral order is seen as
that which guarantees a parallel continuity of the species.
We must try to understand this as operating within
a framework which can conveniently be termed the

metaphysics of the irreducible: knowledge of birth and death as the human cycle; the wind as a moving, felling, cleansing, destroying, winnowing force; the duality of the knife as blood-letter and creative implement; earth and sun as life-sustaining verities, and so on. These serve as matrices within which mores, personal relationships, even communal economics are formulated and reviewed. Other 'irreducible' acceptances may evolve from this; for instance, the laws of hospitality or the taboo on incest, but they do not possess the same strength and compulsion as the fundamental matrix. They belong to a secondary category and may be contradicted by accident or human failing.

The profound experience of tragic drama is comprehensible within such irreducible hermeticism. Because of the visceral intertwining of each individual with the fate of the entire community, a rupture in his normal functioning not only endangers this shared reality but threatens existence itself.

The African world-view is not, however, even by implication, stagnant. This may seem a surprising assertion to those who consider that the kind of society which has emerged from the foregoing fits rather disturbingly into Karl Popper's[5] primitive blueprint for the modern totalitarian society. Popper's uneven knowledge of the societies which he attempts to ease into his specially constructed closed circle has of course been remarked by several of his critics. His fundamental assumptions are inaccurate. They bypass the code on which this world-view is based, the continuing evolution of tribal wisdom through an acceptance of the elastic nature of knowledge as its one reality, as signifying no more than reflections of the original coming-into-being of a manifestly complex reality.[6] European scholars have always betrayed a

[5] Karl Popper, *The Open Society and its Enemies,* Routledge & Kegan Paul, London, 1962.
[6] This is indeed the unifying rationale of the Ifa (Yoruba Divination) corpus.

tendency to accept the myth, the lore, the social tech-
niques of imparting knowledge or of stabilising society as
evidence of orthodox rigidity. Yet the opposite, an attitude of philosophic accommodation, is constantly demonstrated in the attributes accorded most African deities,
attributes which deny the existence of impurities or
'foreign' matter, in the god's digestive system. Experiences which, until the event, lie outside the tribe's
cognition are absorbed through the god's agency, are
converted into yet another piece of the social armoury
in its struggle for existence, and enter the lore of the
tribe. This principle creates for society a non-doctrinaire
mould of constant awareness, one which stays outside the
monopolistic orbit of the priesthood, outside any claims
to gnostic secrets by special cults. Interpretation, as it
does universally, rests mostly in the hands of such in-
termediaries, but rarely with the dogmatic finality of
Christianity or Islam.[7] Their principal function is to
reinforce by observances, rituals and mytho-historical
recitals the existing consciousness of cosmic entangle-
ment in the community, and to arbitrate in the sometimes
difficult application of such truths to domestic and community undertakings.

One other example, a fortunate blend of myth and
history, penetrates even deeper into that area of man's
cosmogonic hunger, one which leads him to the profounder forms of art as retrieval vehicles for, or assertive
links with a lost sense of origin. That the play, *Oba Koso*
is also a tragedy is not deliberate, but it is more than

[7] This accommodative nature, which does not, however, contradict
or pollute their true essences, is what makes Sango capable of extending
his territory of lightning to embrace electricity in the affective consciousness of his followers. Ogun for his part becomes not merely the
god of war but the god of revolution in the most contemporary
context – and this is not merely in Africa, but in the Americas to where
his worship has spread. As the Roman Catholic props of the Batista
regime in Cuba discovered when it was too late, they should have
worried less about Karl Marx than about Ogun, the re-discovered deity
of revolution.

coincidence. Comedy also expresses a world-view, so does melodrama and the other labels of convenience which we attach to drama. But, despite a Molière or a Ben Jonson, even comedies of the archetype must first reduce humanity to the manageable circle of the drama-tist's lens. Tragedy dares to thrust it beyond, suggesting areas of unplumbable mysteries in its passage. It is possible to experience or to penetrate the framework of a world perception from tragedy. Sadly, the would-be tragedies which flood the African literary scene display little of this understanding. Their tawdry claims to at-tention are fulfilled only through momentary frustration at one's inability to refer to available printed plays or to capture in the literary idiom that essence of allegory or symbolic drama which so eloquently consoles man for the limitations that hinder him from grasping, intuitively, the kernels of mysteries that constantly litter his awareness.

Oba Koso[8] straddles the modernist gulf between symbol and expository action and dialogue with the essence of poetry, a perfect unity rarely encountered on the modern African stage. Written and played in Yoruba, it provides a uniquely apposite reference, as it has enjoyed a variety of linguistic audiences all over the world – German, English, Yiddish, Russian, Polish, French etc. – and nowhere has it failed to elicit that profound communal catharsis which is one of the ac-knowledged ends of tragic action. It constitutes a living instance of the universal roots of the tragic pulse and the transcendental nature of *poetry* over the medium of transmission, language, music or movement. One must speak again of the preliminary evocation of a hermetic world, autonomous, demonstrably cohesive, neutral to exterior mores and values, a rich and persuasive

[8] *Oba Koso* is printed in Duro Ladipo, *Three Yoruba Plays* (English adaptation by Ulli Beier), Mbari Publications, Ibadan, 1964. The quotations here are mainly my own translations.

3-2

evocation achieved through the felicitous plurality of the dramatic media, a stylistic and sensual assault both on intimates of that culture and on outsiders equally. A code of meanings is established through rhythm, movement and tonal-specific harmonies which instantly create their own territory of reality. The initiate knows that even the paraphernalia of the protagonists is endowed with significant meanings, social and myth-referential. The outsider senses this with equal certainty and, while he necessarily loses something of the specificity, he is enab-led to create with ease a parallel scale of references since he views it all in the framework of motion and stylised conflict, all obeying a finely regulated rhythm of rela-tionships. He may not, especially if he is tone deaf and chronically arhythmic, appreciate that both rhythm and timbre are also specific and cogent, but his intelligence and sensibility respond to the fact that he is a participant within an integrated matrix of cultural forces, that the tragic unfolding of the reign of Oba Sango is not merely an interesting episode in the annals of a people's history but the spiritual consolidation of the race through immersion in the poetry of origin.

In so far as it is history, the play concerns the machi-nations of a tyrant, Sango, who aims to immobilise one or both of two increasingly powerful warlords in his kingdom. He employs the classic trick of despatching them to keep order on the borders of the kingdom, confident that their matching egos will bring them in fatal conflict with each other. As is usual in these cases, Sango's own counsellors and subjects have themselves egged him on to this course. The ruse fails, however; the two warriors meet and fight, but the victor spares the vanquished. They grow individually more and more powerful. Again, at the insistence of his people, Sango summons them and organises yet another duel. This time the victor, the same one as before, Gbonka, slays his opponent, then turns on the king and demands his

throne. The terrified subjects now act in character, begin
to abandon their king. In a rage at this betrayal he turns
on them and slaughters a few. But the abomination (and
the betrayal) drives him out of the city, and in despair
he hangs himself. Or rather, he does not hang. For the
postscript of the play is his apotheosis and the title of the
play, *Oba Koso* means – the king did not hang. Disgusted
by human fickleness, history declares, Sango ascended
the heavens and joined the other deities of the Yoruba
pantheon.

Here now is a sample of Sango's praise-song; it celebrates his intemperate power and ferocity:

> You think the worm is dancing but
> That is merely the way it walks
> You think Sango is fighting you but
> That is merely the way he is.
>
> He dines on pounded yam with the family head
> Then seizes his first-born on the porch
> And slays him
> He cracks the wall, splits the wall
> He splits it wide open and
> Rams two hundred thunderstones in the crack

But beatific passages of lyricism also abound, prepar-
ing the way for a post-climactic restorative for the race.
The conflict, stylised, drains off the evil energies of
excess. The self-destructive principles embodied in, for
example, the praise-song above, are purged from the
community through the medium of the suffering protagonist. Tragic drama of this nature (and tragic poetry)
operates through the homoeopathic principle, and it
should cause no surprise to find the expression 'praise-
song' applied to such wanton savagery, or to find in
performance that the lines are chanted with a non-critical,
adulatory and joyous involvement. Such passages and
their counterparts are essential to a sense of realistic

health in the community; they embody, it should also be remembered, the conjurative aspects of nature-mysteries and the origin of the race. Invocation of nature's munificence is not a passive operation nor can it be effected by mere pietistic rote. The strength of the community, its insistent will, is written into the poetry of such tragedy. If the protagonist is their symbolic representative through the abyss of origin (racial but also individual), no simplistic moral selectivity can decide what energies may be conjured from nature to aid the emissary. Sango dares the symbolic abyss of transition on behalf of his people, the resources which he calls upon for his passage of terror must be both good and evil. His tragic excess and weakness fulfil the cyclic demand on, and provoke the replenishment of, choric (communal) energies and resilience. It is an eternal tension which is sustained by challenge and response, so thorough and if necessary so 'amoral' that the protagonist is seen as a reflection of that communal strength in all its mottled nature.

This sense of origin, the coming-into-being of the race, dominates the drama. Thus Timi, one of the manipulated generals arrives for the first time at his new settlement – yet another paradigm of origin that poetry insinuates into the action. A total stranger, isolated and apprehensive, he invokes universal aid through his song:

I come this day to Ede town
It is the gentle wind that says, blow towards me
Spirits of teeming termites say, swarm towards me
Air is the Father of Dew
Dew is the Father of Showers
Showers are the Father of the Ocean
Ocean is Father of long-trodden Earth

His appeal, primarily addressed to the as yet unseen inhabitants of Ede, is expanded to trigger awake the animal and spirit world and all Nature's forces, linking them to him through the sympathetic memory of their own origin. The resulting strength of acceptance that he must derive from a favourable response is an echo of similar beneficence derived by the existing inhabitants; it is also a renewal for them. His prayer was once their prayer of appeasement to unseen forces on first invading the once virgin soil. The response of the unseen chorus, in whom all denizens of this undemarcated world are now symbolically fused is therefore emotionally experienced as a re-enactment of their own birth and origin. The tribulations of wandering and settling, of uprooting and displacement, join with this representation of human loneliness and alienation, sensations which lie at the emotional root of tragedy. Timi's song is a summons on man and nature for the remedial aid of acceptance, and the key to unlock this source of strength is the mythopoeic evocation of the passage of race.

> I come this day to Ede town
> It is the gentle wind that says, blow towards me
> Spirits of swarming termites say, swarm towards me
> Two hundred rafters support the house
> Two hundred lizards support the wall
> Let all hands be raised to sustain me...

Like the preceding passage, the constant thread is – continuity. Timi's struggle is presented as inseparable from the evidence of Nature at its most domestic. It merges into the larger universe of wind, rain and ocean, growth and regeneration, a humanistic faith and affirmation which is the other face of tragic loss. So even this lesser character, no less than Gbonka, no less than the choric compact, no less than Sango himself, is protagonist of continuity, skirting the rim of that heart of cosmic mysteries into which his leader Sango will shortly plunge.

Located in the poignant moments of the race's coming-into-being, the terrain has nonetheless grown familiar and pertinent even to the alien participant in these tragic

59

rites of origin. This is because *Oba Koso* confidently asserts its own laws of cohesive interiority. It expands thereafter through the jubilant accents of poetry and passion to a retrieval of the enlarged consciousness of being, universal and individual.

3

Ideology and the social vision
(1): The religious factor

Asked recently whether or not I accepted the necessity
for a literary ideology, I found myself predictably exa-
mining the problem from the inside, that is, from within
the consciousness of the artist in the process of creating.
It was a familiar question, one which always reappears
in multiple guises. My response was – a social vision, yes,
but not a literary ideology. Generally the question reflects
the preoccupation, neither of the traditional nor the
contemporary writer in African society but of the analyst
after the event, the critic. An examination of the works
of most contemporary writers confirms this. But then, it
would be equally false to suggest that contemporary
African literature is not consciously formulated around
certain frameworks of ideological intent. The problem
is partly one of terminology and the associations of
literary history, mostly European. The danger which a
literary ideology poses is the act of consecration – and of
course excommunication. Thanks to the tendency of the
modern consumer-mind to facilitate digestion by putting
in strict categories what are essentially fluid operations
of the creative mind upon social and natural phenomena,
the formulation of a literary ideology tends to congeal
sooner or later into instant capsules which, administered
also to the writer, may end by asphixiating the creative
process. Such a methodology of assessment does not
permit a non-prejudicial probing of the capsule itself, at
least not by the literature which brings it into being or
which it later brings into being. Probing, if there is any,
is an incestuous activity on its own, at least until the
fabrication of a rival concept. It is easy to see that this

process can only develop into that in-breeding which offers little objective enlightenment about its nature, since its idiom and concepts are not freed from the ideology itself. When the reigning ideology fails finally to retain its false comprehensive adequacy, it is discarded. A new set, inviolable mould is fabricated to contain the current body of literature or to stimulate the next along predetermined patterns.

There may appear to be contrary instances to invalidate the suggestion that literary ideologies are really the conscious formulation of the critic, not the artist. But this contradiction exists only when we take as our frame of reference – which regrettably still seems the automatic thing to do – European literary experience. The idea of literature as an objective existence in itself is a very European idea, and ideologies are very much systems of thought or speculative goals considered desirable for the health of existing institutions (society, ecology, economic life etc.) which are, or have come to be regarded as, ends in themselves. Take the French Surrealist movement: even while paying lip-service to the claims of literature as an expression of an end (the infinity of human experience), the Surrealists laboured, by their obsessive concentration on the ontology of a creative medium (in their case literature) to set the medium apart as an autogenous phenomenon, so cutting it off from the human phenomenon which it is supposed to reflect, or on behalf of which it is supposed to speculate. Perhaps it came from taking far too literally the annunciation of the Gospel – In the beginning was the *Word*. Similar claims for the objective existence of the medium are even more overtly stated in the other arts, painting especially. Since we have no experience of such distortions of objective relationships in African society, it is reasonable to claim that a literary ideology traditionally has had little to do with the actual process of creating that literature. In contemporary times there has been

one important exception to this pattern, apart from
lesser related efforts which periodically attempt to
bring the direction of African writing under a fiat of
instant-assimilation poetics.

Some literary ideologies take private hallucinatory
forms. Samuel Beckett, for instance, gropes incessantly
towards the theatrical statement that can be made in one
word, a not-too-distant blood-relation of the chimeric
obsessions of the Surrealists. If we leave the lunatic fringe
of the literary Unilateral Declaration of Independence,
however, we discover that despite its tendency towards
narrow schematism, a literary ideology does occasionally
achieve coincidence – and so a value expansion – with a
social vision. From merely turning the mechanics of
creativity into a wilful self-regulating domain, irrespective of the burden of statement, it elevates its sights to
a regenerative social goal which makes continuing demands on the nature of that ideological medium and
prevents its smug stagnation. Brecht's ideology of theatre
and dramatic literature is the most successful example.
A not-so-successful instance was the French neo-fiction
movement of the fifties which rejected metaphorical
language for a bare diction of objective reality, this being
for its practitioners a necessary aid to the conditioning
of a social consciousness. Alas, the energy and passion
of social revolution appears perversely to quarry into the
metaphorical resources of language in order to brand its
message deeper in the heart of humanity: the products
of that movement now largely belong to the literary
museum. It was, however, a far cry from the purely
stylistic and intellectual preoccupations of its distant
forerunner, the eighteenth-century European Enlightenment, whose ideology of literature all but re-defined
poetry and tragic drama out of imaginative existence. In
Africa, Negritude remains the only claimant to this
fruitful coincidence. The concept of a socio-racial direction governed a whole literary ideology and gave it its

choice of mode of expression and thematic emphasis. Both for Africans on the mother-continent and for the black societies of the diaspora, Negritude provided both a life-line along which the dissociated individual could be pulled back to the source of his matrical essence, and offered a prospect for the coming-into-being of new black social entities. In the process it enmeshed itself unnecessarily in negative contradictory definitions. We shall deal more fully with the phenomenon of Negritude in our encounter with the development of a secular social vision.

I have said already that all this must not be taken to mean that contemporary literature in Africa is not consciously guided by concepts of an ideological nature. But the writer is far more preoccupied with visionary projection of society than with speculative projections of the nature of literature, or of any other medium of expression. The ontology of the idiom is subservient to the burden of its concerns; yet there is no record of periods of total literary atrophy in societies that boast a recognisable literary tradition. This is because, in reality, the umbilical chord between experience and form has never been severed, no matter how tautly stretched. But the reflection of experience is only one of the functions of literature; there is also its extension. And when that experience is social we move into areas of ideological projections, the social vision. It is this latter form of literature that holds the most promise for the strengthening of the bond between experience and medium since it prevents the entrenchment of the habitual, the petrification of the imaginative function by that past or present reality upon which it reflects. Literature of a social vision is not a perfect expression for this dimension of creative writing but it will serve for the moment, for want of a better. Yambo Oulouguem's *Le Devoir de Violence* is one paradoxical example of such a literature; it is purposely introduced at this stage in order to

crystallise through its example that most important function of the genre, the decongealment of the imaginative
function by past or present reality, even in the process
of reflecting upon them. The claims of a literary ideology
are related but the practical effects on the creative
process lead to predictability, imaginative constraint, and
thematic excisions.

It will be necessary also to suspend our habitual prejudices in our approach to this literature. The expression
'social vision' is chosen as a convenient delimitation for
certain types of literature to be discussed, not as an
elevated concept of the type. 'Vision' is a word which has
strong connotations of the lofty and the profound, and
this tends to rub off on literature which lays claim to it.
This, of course, is not necessarily the case. A novelette
like Alex la Guma's *A Walk in the Night* (Mbari Publications, 1964) makes no social visionary claims but restricts
itself to a near obsessive delineation of the physical,
particularised reality of a South African ghetto existence.
Yet its total statement both about the reality of that
situation and on the innate regressive capacity of man
in a dehumanised social condition provides a more
profound and disturbing insight into humanity than we
find in the visionary piety of his fellow country man Alan
Paton or the multi-racial vision of Peter Abrahams. A
demand which I once made in a paper that the writer
in our modern African society needs to be a visionary in
his own times has, I find, been often interpreted as a
declaration that this is the highest possible function for
the contemporary African writer. The misunderstanding has to do with the elevated status which the European
mind inclines to give to works of a mystical or visionary
persuasion – witness the way in which the dotty excursions of W. B. Yeats into a private never-never land are
reverently exegetised! Let it be noted that in a culture
where the mystical and the visionary are merely areas of
reality like any other, the use of such expressions does

not connote a higher perception of the imaginative faculty.

A creative concern which conceptualises or extends actuality beyond the purely narrative, making it reveal realities beyond the immediately attainable, a concern which upsets orthodox acceptances in an effort to free society of historical or other superstitutions, these are qualities possessed by literature of a social vision. Revolutionary writing is generally of this kind, though whether or not much of the writing which aspires to the label is always literature is another question. Sembene Ousmane's *God's Bits of Wood* leaves one in no doubt about its literary qualities, and combines revolutionary fervour with a distinctly humanist vision. The intellectual and imaginative impulse to a re-examination of the propositions on which man, nature and society are posited or interpreted at any point in history; the effort to expand such propositions, or to contest and replace them with others more in tune with the writer's own idealistic disposition or his pragmatic, resolving genius; this impulse and its integrative role in the ordering of experience and events leads to a work of social vision. A literary ideology and social vision may meet in particular modes of creative expression – they do, certainly, in the literature of Negritude, in Brecht's epic theatre and (with the usual reservations) in the dramatic literature of European Expressionism. (The amorphous, even contradictory and unruly nature of some products of the conscious marriage of ideology and form can be seen in this last example. Not many analysts of that Expressionist ferment will disagree with Gorelik, who said: '. . . just what Expressionism meant was rather puzzling to its reviewers at the time and in fact is not entirely clear to this day.') With such occasional productive concurrence of a literary ideology and a social vision in mind, it is possible to claim that the lack of excessive stylistic contrivance in modern African literature is due to the refusal of the artist to respond to the blandishments of literary ideology-manifesto art. Much African writing is still rooted in the concept of literature as part of the normal social activity of man, but one which is nonetheless individual in its expression and its choice of areas of concern. That writing which claims for itself, subtly or stridently, the poet's famous province – unacknowledged legislators of mankind – with or without the poetry or the poetic insight, is always socially significant. For it gives clues to mental conditioning by previous history or colonial culture; or conversely shows the will to break free of such incubi in its projection of a future society. The literature which devotes itself to this area is a revelation both of the individual sensibility of the writers and of the traditional and colonial background of Africa's contemporary reality.

It is best to begin with the less memorable instances. One of the earlier novels of the sixties, *The African,* was written by a Gambian, William Conton.[1] Simplistically autobiographical (in the fleshing out, not in the actual dramatic events) it tells the story of an African student in Britain who meets and falls in love with a white South African girl. The love is reciprocated – why, it is difficult to say, as our hero Kamara is an unbelievable prig, bore, a glutton for humiliation and what the Afro-American would call a self-excusing nigger. Supposed flashes of indignation emerge prim or wet, couched in a language of propriety which our hero conceives as cultured repartee. Such language is offered without apparent criticism; there is no ironical intention when the hero utters this caricature of European drawing-room discourse. Thus, after he has been accurately insulted with the word 'nigger', flung at him by the girl's fiancé, another white South African, his reactions emerge as follows:

[1] William Conton, *The African,* Heinemann, London, 1960.

The word 'nigger' is one deeply resented by all
Africans who know it. Nothing will deprive us of
our self-restraint so rapidly as the use of it, whether
by an adult or, as so often by an unmannerly
English child. I felt my temper rising rapidly. There
was only one thing to be done, and quickly.

'I have enough respect for the presence among
us of a lady not to help *you* to your true place with
my fists, Mr Hertog. You have insulted me deeply
and deliberately, without the slightest provocation
on my part, and before we were even introduced. I
am, I assure you, only too glad to take my leave of a
person of ill-breeding.' (*The African,* p. 72)

Having done quickly what needed to be done, the black
preux chevalier proceeds to take his leave. Perhaps the
author, feeling that he had exposed the reader to as
much as he can take, had decided to give him a breathing-
space; but Kamara is by no means finished. The author's
sole concession to this uncritical abuse of language comes
in a mild, indulgent self-mockery:

I turned to go; then found I had enjoyed saying
this much, and could not resist the temptation to
practise my English rhetoric a little further. (p. 72)

Upon which Kamara issues a challenge which is of course
contemptuously ignored, rounds it off with a pathetically
feeble witticism, and takes his leave feeling, he declares,
'unaccountably elated'.

The example is sufficient to show that William Conton
has recreated the colonial milksop and tried to pass him
off as noble and dignified. It is hardly surprising, but
nevertheless alarming, that the author returns this same
character to his country, turns him into a hero of the
independence struggle and makes him his nation's first
Prime Minister. One could say, perhaps, that William
Conton's work contained a prophetic warning on the

nature of the first crop of Africa's post-independence leaders, except of course that the portrait appears to be more wishful prayer than prophetic warning.

Before Kamara's triumphant return, however, a tragedy scars his life for ever. Hertog, the outraged fiancé, deliberately runs down the lovers in his car, kills the girl and injures the hero. Lying in his hospital bed, Kamara formulates a vow of revenge. He returns home first, and is revealed as a great patriot, nationalist and traditionalist; that is, he abandons 'Christian' ways and turns to his parents to choose him a bride. He turns his back on the acquisitive ethic that has eaten into the fabric of his people, the material and cultural corruption brought upon them by the incursion of Western ideas, Hollywood trivia and vulgarity. In his campaign-speeches he attacks the colonial capitalist monopoly and demands quick independence. He re-discovers his own people, his own heritage, undergoes a rebirth, so to speak, and takes to wearing traditional clothes. His political vision embraces a United States of Africa. He has all the right reactions to apartheid, his revulsion at the sight of photographs of Africans brutalised by the police is violent and passionate; we have no doubt that he would eat any white African upholder of apartheid alive if he ever got the chance.

He soon provides himself with that chance. For after a number of rather amazing, even quixotic preparations, considering the fact that he is Prime Minister and could have made things a lot easier for himself, he sets out incognito for South Africa on his odyssey of vengeance. In spite of two loving and loyal wives, in spite of his visionary politics and the responsibilities of government, in spite of the passing years, he has not forgotten this original vow and he sets out in pursuit of the murderer of his beloved. He makes his journey successfully. He locates his enemy and finally has him at his mercy, drunk and incapacitated. But,

as the first drums began to send their throbbing
message out across the night it was pity I found in
my heart for him, not hate. I stopped quickly, lifted
him gently, and bore him through the easy rain to
the safety of his home. (p. 213)

It is difficult to resist a counter-scene – our hero stopped
by a white policeman who demands what he is doing with
a white body in his black African arms. The lessons would
be well deserved. As an adventure story, this work would
be pardonable, but *The African* aspires beyond this,
beyond the narrative and actualities to a summative
humanistic statement on the lines of forgiveness and
reconciliation. The title itself indicates that the author is
promoting a desired representative of the African Personality, a knowledgeable spokesman built up through
identification with applaudable political and cultural
goals. His vision of a United States of Africa, of a
Songhaian egalitarian social structure cleansed of corruption and greed, is however swallowed up by what can
be summed up as a rather obvious piece of propaganda
for Christian ideology – turn the other cheek; forgive
thine enemies; return good for evil etc. Presumably these
are the ethical lines on which an envisioned regeneration
of society will be based. Using the agency of trans-
continental epic, symbolising in one person all that is
noble, pure and authentically African (including perhaps
the Islamic bent of the hero?) we are offered a vision of
a continent whose murderous contradictions will be
resolved through a Christian generosity of mind.

The drama offers us another example of this hankering
for a Christian salvationist ethic – the love variety. The
play is *Rhythms of Violence*[2] by, strangely enough, a

[2] Much of the following commentary on this play was first made in
a lecture 'Drama and the Revolutionary Ideal' delivered at the University of Washington, Seattle. *Rhythms of Violence* was published by
Oxford University Press, 1964.

South African, Lewis Nkosi. It is the dream of a love-sick revolutionary conspirator whose infatuation for a white girl brings disaster on his group. The message appears to be that a multi-racial society is the ideal goal for South Africa (which no one denies), and in this play we are given a makeshift instance of that idyllic possibility. The principle is neither original nor banal, neither utopian nor pessimist. But Nkosi's entire projection of the future breaks down over the nature of that proof, a self-immolating proof which the disinherited of society appear required to provide to justify their worthiness to participate in the realisation of the vision. Or perhaps (it all depends how one interprets Lewis Nkosi's goals) it is the very act of bringing such a vision into reality that is made to depend on perpetual self-sacrifice by the down-trodden. 'And from him who hath nothing, even that little which he hath...' Nkosi appears anxious to assure his audience of the unlimited capacity of black human-ism. But this example owes less to the phenomenon of beginning to believe in one's own myths – as with William Conton's negritudinous variant – than to a total alienation from reality and a misunderstanding of the nature and demands of true tragedy. *Make love not war* ...Flower Power is a reformist notion which, apart from presupposing the existence of parks and gardens, also assumes a rudimentary knowledge in the armed opposi-tion of the symbolism of flowers. There are no flowers in the South African ghetto, and the apartheid species of inhumanity sees flowers merely as a reflection of its own civilisation. To stick a rose into the end of a gun muzzle held by a National Guard before the White House is one thing; to transfer this cossetted revolutionary culture to the completely arid environment of apartheid and hope that it will not only flourish in the secret cellars of liberalism but can actually defuse the time-bomb of apartheid is a highly dangerous piece of propaganda. The love optimism of Nkosi's play is grafted on; the idiom of the tragedy of liberal encounter is artificial and untenable.

And as would-be tragedy, the play does not even attempt to create a credibly hermetic milieu within which the trapped individual can be observed in his dilemma. We are denied a dialectic of the social situation, the metaphor of the illogic that makes up their logic, the symbols of inhumanity that constitute their humanity, the procession of untruths that legislates the truths of the society. The question is not whether, as Africans or would-be revolutionaries, we are repelled by the mawk-ishness of a dilemma that is so posed. The problem is essentially the insubstantiality of the 'tragic hero' and the somophoric level of the dialogue that carries forward the dramatic action. The age of the characters – and this is largely a teenage gathering – need not preclude the necessary depth of language or of feeling. Wedekind's sensitive self-projection into youthful self-discovery, the absorption of his schoolboy characters in a private and internally congruent world created in *Spring Awakening* a poignant tragedy of adolescence. Nkosi's world is neither one of discovery nor of sacrifice; it is neither (though these are its implicit aims) the world of love, nor of revolution. The soil in which he seeks to plant the seed of tragedy is the mere dust of circumstantial events.

There is a warning in all this for the would-be social visionary. It is not necessary to go so far as to accept Trotsky's principle that all literature written in a situation of revolutionary confrontation cannot but be imbued with the spirit of social hatred.[3] It is logical, however, to expect that all literature which sets out to depict the realities of such a situation must reflect that social hatred in the components of the resolution. There are unques-tionably areas of contrasting awareness even in the most intense moments of social convulsion, and the human

[3] Leon Trotsky, *Literature and Revolution,* University of Michigan Press, 1971.

spirit is not impoverished by a faithful reflection of these very special and quiescent areas. But writing directed at the product of a social matrix must expect to remain within it, and to resolve the conflicts which belong to that milieu by the logical interactions of its components, one cannot stand outside of it all and impose a pietistic resolution plucked from some rare region of the artist's uncontaminated soul. To paraphrase Trotsky, we cannot tear out of the future that which can only develop as an inseparable part of it and hurriedly materialise this partial anticipation in present-day dirt and before the cold footlights. To do this is not to be a visionary but to be starry-eyed.

My response to these samples of the literature of reconciliation must not be taken to mean a cynical approach to the principle itself. Richard Rive is another South African, and his play *Make like Slaves*[4] is one fortunate example of a credible creative expression of the longing for humane resolution along the lines of reconciliation. But Richard Rive's resolution demands a reciprocal, intelligent understanding among the embattled parties. The play offers a mordant dissection of a specialised category of the same racial situation and reveals, in a more subtle and effective way, some thread of hope for the breakdown of racial barriers. He does this by the paradox of confronting reality; indeed at the end it is possible to surmise that he suggests the impossibility of resolution. But the integrity of his treatment is revealed by the fact that he inscribes over this failure the fact of individual shortcomings. We are left to feel that, given a more sensitive white woman or a less abrasive (and guilt-ridden) coloured man, given indeed time for the continuation of a process which has begun in the play – the process of self-examination and the recovery of the ability to see individuals as opposed to groups – a small

---

[4] In G. Henderson and C. Pieterse (eds.), *Nine African Plays for Radio*, Heinemann, London, 1974.

part of the battle would be won. The strength of Richard Rive's writing is that he does not exaggerate the pace of this process, nor does he anywhere suggest that, if a negative, external event were interjected into this evolutionary process it would not, at least for the duration of that event, halt or distort the tempo of the positive development. And even that awareness, hovering in the background, its pity, gives more value to the gains that have been made.

And a similar level of awareness, of self-caution without pandering, is expressed in an unusual poem by Denis Brutus, unusual in being unlike his usual indictment of the racial situation. It operates from the pessimistic perspective of the common guilt-potential of humanity, successfully skirting the precipice of a possible betrayal of one's own cause. The common humanity – that negative aspect – to which he gives expression is not seen as a distant likelihood but as an uncomfortable, existing reality. A cautionary moment in an otherwise predictable self-representation within the trapped ranks of the oppressed, it reveals the poet as a sensibility which engages the present, but simultaneously envisages the social harvest of struggle. The humanity that will people the future is not to be left until the future, not to be taken for granted nor indulged in later through an expedient justification of its crimes:

> Their guilt
> is not so very different from ours:
> – who has not joyed in the arbitrary exercise of
> power
> or grasped for himself what might have been
> another's
> and who has not used superior force in the moment
> when he could
> (and who of us has not been tempted to these
> things?) –

74

so, in their guilt,
the bared ferocity of teeth,
chest-thumping challenge and defiance,
the deafening clamour of their prayers
to a deity made in the image of their prejudice
which drowns the voice of conscience,
is mirrored our predicament...[5]

It is an expression of the bleak intimations that must result from an uncompromising stare at the common denominators of humanity. Glared at in its turn from an uncompromising revolutionary stance it may appear to cross the edge of blasphemy, for it is possible to claim that the expression of such insights (and the negative compassion it entails) is a palliative to the unrepentant conscience of criminal power possessed by the white social oppressor; or at the best, it could become a gratuitous *mea culpism* which enervates the revolutionary will. It is healthiest, however, to accept such insights fully and on their own terms, to regard them as a realistic and essential dimension of the moral equipment required for the reconstruction not merely of society but of man. It is hard and unsentimental, an inward-directed demand for self-cognition, quite different from the dangerous hara-kiri humanism of Nkosi's play. But the final argument lies simply in the treacherous reality of today's self-governing African nations. Nothing more starkly damning is required than a casual dissection of the reality of power on the continent. 'The deity made in the image of their prejudice' can no longer be identified along the simplistic colour line.

It is customary to think primarily of Christian ideology when the question of religious influence (on ethics, language, and so on) is posed in the context of modern

---

[5] From 'Their Behaviour', footnoted 'Blood River Day, 1965', in *A Simple Lust*, Heinemann, London, 1973, p. 79.

African literature. Because of the background of the majority of the better-known authors and the general orientation of much African literary practice towards the Christian West, it is sometimes forgotten that there is also an important proportion of the literary output whose inspiration derives from a non-Christian world-view, most notably that of Islam. Either in self-contained form, that is, springing entirely from and resolved within an Islamic frame of reference – Cheikh Hamidou Kane's *L'Aventure Ambiguë* is one useful example of that – or, as a reaction against the Christian presence, deploying aggressive or subtle influences upon African indigenous values, the Islamic vision has played a fertile role in the literary creations of the last century.

We must differentiate first of all between the deliberate use of Christian or Islamic symbolism, metaphors or historic archetypes, and the application of the ideologies of such major religions where a particular religious ethic may coat a literary work and dominate its resolution. The poet Tchikaya U'Tamsi, for example, belongs to the first group. It is typical of this poet to attempt to convey his sense of affronted humanity at, for instance, the murder and mutilation of the black boy Emmett Till in the United States, through images of the crucified Christ and a Congolese saint, Saint Anne of the Congo. That poem, and the writing of U'Tamsi in general, thrives on a dense religious eclecticism. On the Islamic side, Malik Fall also belongs to the same group as U'Tamsi in the tradition of distilling the components of a religious culture and permeating a social milieu with its essence. His allegorical work *The Wound* (Heinemann, 1973) is a quasi-mystical novel of this genre. It is a parable of human identity, a search for self, a transcendence of the limitations of mortality tied to the all too human craving for the basic security of mortal acceptance, narrated against the background of colonial cultural supersession.

However, it is the works in the second category which

really concern us here. And first, a work which is indeed one of direct unapologetic proselytising. In colonial societies which constantly seek a world-view to challenge the inherent iniquities of any philosophy which can be associated with the colonial intrusion, we naturally encounter works which make a point of claiming that Islam – a very effective organised challenge to Christian cultural authority – is one religion whose ethics, philosophy and form of worship reconciles races and encourages universal fraternalism. Hampate Ba's *Tierno Bokar* is a very persuasive biography of a Muslim sage, the Sage of Bandiagara.[6] At the basis of Tierno Bokar's teaching is the simple message of a universal humanism, a belief in an eventual tolerance and mutual generosity of sufficient strength to transcend historic memory. No doubt it is this hankering for understanding at any cost, this search for the leaven of reconciliation, that occasionally produces the rather misguided literature that we began by discussing. One difference is obvious: *Tierno Bokar* is a straightforward biography. It narrates the religious apprenticeship and the growth of wisdom in an individual whose largeness of vision enables him, even while lauding the superiority of Islam over Christianity, to preach the accommodation of the rival faith within the spirit of tolerance. What is significant to our theme is Hampate Ba's studied attention to the life of the Moslem sage. It is an integral part of several works designed to counter the Christian colonial culture of African experience with another cultural force from within the heritage of the society. The language itself, its meticulous exposition, is a clue to the absolute concurrence of ideals espoused by the author and his chosen subject, the acceptance of the burden of transmission of the message of the Master, rendered explicit in his teaching and implicit in his life. Hampate Ba writes:

[6] Hampate Ba and Marcel Cardaire, *Tierno Bokar, le Sage de Bandiagara,* Presence Africaine, 1957.

At last, with all his lucidity, Tierno had taken full
measure of the disequilibrium from which the
entire African society suffers. Dare we say that the
ill has become aggravated since the Master made
this assertion in an age when it ought to be able to
pass now as prophecy of what was to come? Drawn
by several centres of attraction, Africa is diverted
along lines of forces which tear away its members
from their original place. We will not revert to the
opinion which the master had of this derangement,
understood in the religious sense. It seemed to him
supremely ridiculous. Understood in the most
general sense of a cultural disintegration, the
phenomenon from which the African society suffers
seems infinitely tiresome to the Sage of Bandiagara,
who knows only too well that the remedy is in the
cultural foundation of the races themselves. (*Tierno
Bokar,* p. 90, author's translation)

This, then, is the real purpose of Hampate Ba's study
of Tierno Bokar: to expand the sage's observations on
that Africa which has resulted from the impact of alien
civilisation into a critique of contemporary society, and
to provide a philosophic basis for the construction of a
new one, a larger, more stable brotherhood through the
acceptance of the truth of Islam. Here is another passage
of the Sage's direct catechising:

Today this word is breaking out of the narrow
limits in which it has remained. We offer it to the
public. The last paragraph of this chapter, devoted
to the Message cannot be from us. Once again we
make way for Tierno Bokar:
  'I look forward with all my heart to the era of
reconciliation between all the creeds on earth, era
when these united faiths will support each other to
form a canopy, the era when they will rest in God

on three points of support: Love, Charity and
Fraternity.'[7]

This, let it be remembered, was at least forty years before
the tentative efforts of the Vatican to effect a reconciliation, not of course with non-Christian religions, but with
the various pieces which broke away when the Rock of
St Peter began to crack.

The philosophic fiction of Cheikh Hamidou Kane,
L'Aventure Ambigüe,[8] is in a very different class of
writing, far less didactic but pervaded more deeply by
the mystical aura of Islam. Its mission is sustained by a
vision of mankind, and more specifically, of a new
African consciousness shaped by the wisdom of Islam
and a sensibility that occasionally, very occasionally,
suggests the animism of African traditional beliefs:

> You have not only raised yourself above Nature.
> You have even turned the sword of your thought
> against her: You are fighting for her subjection –
> that is your combat, isn't it? I have not yet cut the
> umbilical cord which makes me one with her. The
> supreme dignity to which, still today, I aspire is to
> be the most sensitive and the most filial part of her.
> Being Nature herself, I do not dare to fight against
> her. I never open up the bosom of the earth, in
> search of my food, without demanding pardon,
> trembling, beforehand. I never strike a tree,
> coveting its body, without fraternal supplication to
> it. I am only that end of being where thought comes
> to flower.

The emphasis is, however, on Islam. The contest for
the soul of Samba Diallo, a contest which began in his
childhood against the demands of secularism and spreads

[7] Translation in Claude Wauthier, *The Literature and Thought of
Modern Africa*, Pall Mall, London, 1966, p. 231.
[8] Cheikh Hamidou Kane, *Ambiguous Adventure*, Heinemann,
London, 1972.

in later maturity to the more complex and precarious arena of Europe, is waged on behalf of an Islamic vision of being. The godlessness that is Europe is an implacable ogre: 'I have learnt that in the country of the white man, the revolt against poverty and misery is not distinguished from the revolt against God. They say that the movement is spreading, and that soon the same great cry against poverty will drown out the voice of the muezzins.' The humane motivation that brought Communism into existence as an irresistible social force is prejudicially acknowledged to facilitate the purpose of its self-indictment. The charge is impiety, the verdict a foregone conclusion. The human spirit is endangered; this is the summation of discourse among the Diallobe's learned and wise. Metaphor and imagery reinforce the bias – what chance has the pejoratively evoked image of hammer and sickle against the star and the crescent, against the replete immediacy of Kane's Glowing Hearth?

That quality of the language of the Koran which Kane describes as a 'sombre beauty' he tries consciously to capture in his own prose. The quality comes out even in translation, cleanly sculpted yet mysterious and often elusive, suggestive of much that is left unspoken, layers of perception that need paring away. No criticism of the manic excesses of the Teacher of the Text is permitted to creep into the writing; his explicit sadism (a familiar feature not only of Koranic teachers but of the traditional village schoolmaster) is subsumed in the Teacher's great love, the mystic purity of his motives; torture by blazing faggots is the 'incandescence' of the Text. Given into the hands of the Muslim sage for instruction, Samba Diallo masters the Word, learns the virtues of humility by subsisting, with other pupils, solely on charity. Perfection is sought constantly, even in the art of begging: 'In the name of God, give to those who beg for his glory. Men who sleep, think of the disciples passing by!' The moral insertions are phrased with a lyricism that seeks to replace the missing oral flow of the marabouts: 'Men of God, death is not that night which traitorously floods with darkness the innocent and lively ardour of a summer day. It warns, then it mows down in the full mid-day of the intelligence.' Even the teacher is impressed by Diallo's improvisations. He calls them 'beautiful and profound'. Hamidou Kane is a diligent expositor of the Faith.

At last, Samba Diallo, for whom even a physical fight is controlled and experienced as a kind of mystic choreography culminating in a catharsis of body and mind, leaves his homeland to grapple with more formidable foes than an envious fellow pupil. The contest is more than individual. The crises of decision already revealed in the leadership of the Diallobe – the Most Royal Lady, the Chief of the Diallobe, the Teacher – have involved the future of entire generations in the personal odyssey of Samba Diallo, yet the hero's inner conflicts are intensely individual and spiritual. His chosen subject, philosophy, facilitates exposition of the contested ground. We have already listened to his father and Monsieur Lacroix in a well-matched contest over the truths of their separate worlds. There, Diallo's mission, his destiny, is defined in staggering pan-ethnic terms with a sonorous invocation of cosmic arbiters that sounds excessively impassioned:

'Do not do violence to yourself, M. Lacroix! I know that you do not believe in the shade; nor in the end of the world. What you do not see does not exist. The moment, like a raft, carries you on the luminous surface of its round disc, and you deny the abyss, from which will come great gusts of shadow upon our shrivelled bodies, our haggard brows. With all my soul I wish for this opening. In the city which is being born such should be our work – all of us, Hindus, Chinese, South Americans, Negroes, Arabs, all of us, awkward and pitiful, we

81

the under-developed, who feel ourselves to be clumsy in a world of perfect mechanical adjustment...' (*Ambiguous Adventure,* p. 80)

'God in Whom I believe, if we are not to succeed, let the Apocalypse come! Take away from us that liberty of which we shall have known how to make use. May Thy hand fall heavily, then, upon the great unconsciousness. May the arbitrary power of Thy will throw out of order the stable course of our laws...' (p. 81)

From within his profoundly Muslim personality, Diallo manifests the quintessence of African humanity and the destiny of the black race. The materialist atheism of the West is assaulted with the West's own dialectical weapons. His individual loneliness and the precariousness of his role is underscored by encounters with degenerate negroes who have fallen victim to the blasphemies of Europe. The humanity survives but another price has been extorted from Diallo; he experiences god-abandonment, his faith becomes uncertain.

Through it all runs a secondary thread; one that does not, however, occupy a level of secondary relevance but could indeed, depending on individual inclination, be regarded as a crucial theme of the work. An obsession with death and mortality has been the basis of the Teacher's instructions to his pupil; it is to stay with Diallo for the rest of his short life and indeed to colour both his spiritual and intellectual approach to existence. Mortality, decay and transience have become the focus of perception – thought, matter and phenomenon are made relative to this centre of reality and, recalling the Teacher's own preparation for death, there is a temptation to consider that Samba Diallo has been used (and warped) by the Teacher in what is his own personal battle. The Teacher's conversation with the Royal Lady on the subject is very revealing. Her objections are overridden, but the opposed arguments are hardly objective. The turbid vision of existence to which the Teacher exposes a seven-year-old child earns our sympathy for the woman's insistence on the positive in life; a different reading and a re-location of the centrality of themes makes this a key scene and a disquieting one. *Ambiguous Adventure* suggests, from this other perspective, the waste of a sensitive and spiritual individual whose social fulfilment has been sacrificed to an old man's quest for death-serenity. In the view of the Faith this would be an acceptable offering. The Teacher has embodied the Word, 'he has the Word, which is made of nothing corporeal but which endures...' It is consistent that he has championed the virtues of the negation of the social being against the Royal Lady's insistence on social usefulness. 'As for me', declares Diallo in Paris, 'I do not fight for liberty, but for God.' The paradoxes in Diallo's understanding of God are perhaps responsible for the following interpretation: that because he strives to see God as the ultimate attainment, death and corruption – being also the ultimate attainment – have become fused in his inner awareness with God. It is hard to escape this conclusion, given confessions like this one from the anguished youth:

> 'It seems to me, for example, that in the country of the Diallobe man is closer to death. He lives on more familiar terms with it. His existence acquires from it something like an aftermath of authenticity. Down there, there existed between death and myself an intimacy.' (p. 149)

And a moment later:

> 'It still seems to me that in coming here I have lost a privileged mode of acquaintance...No scholar ever had such knowledge of anything as I had, then, of being...Here, now, the world is silent and

there is no longer any resonance from myself. I am like a broken balafong, like a musical instrument that has gone dead.' (p. 150)

Can this language be separated from his later expressions of the feeling of god-abandonment?

'The scene is the same. It has to do with the same house, hemmed in by a sky more or less blue, a countryside more or less animated, water running, trees growing, men and animals living there. The scene is the same, I still recognise it.

Lucienne, that scene, it is a sham! Behind it, there is something a thousand times more beautiful, a thousand times more true! But I can no longer find that world's pathway.' (p. 144)

His mutterings during his early necrophilic excursions also complement his Teacher's dicta on the theme. To the Princess's protest that the new generation will have to do with the world of the living, that the values of death will be scoffed at and regarded as bankrupt, the Teacher declares: 'No, Madame. Those are the ultimate values, which will still have their place at the pillow of the last human being.' An effective play on words and temporal associations, which nevertheless begs the question. When life is apprehended solely through its negation, death, existence becomes defined as a temporal illusion; Diallo's crisis of belief is the familiar crisis of one who sees existence as meaningless and the desired reality as elusive. His death at the hands of the Fool now makes sense: it is both symbolic and logical – within the logic of all drama of the absurd wherein the human component of a social architecture is displaced and deprived of a bearing, of significant or meaningful relations. Diallo, would-be 'artisan' of the citadel against the Western abyss, has somehow permitted the weakening of his foundation. It is appropriate that he should be slain by a waywards splinter from the crumbling edifice.

84

What emerges triumphant? This orientation of emphasis towards the metaphor of contest is by no means comprehensive, but it is inevitable from the point of view of our overall theme. The victor is not traditional Diallobe society, nor the West which was responsible for the weakening of Diallo's spiritual roots, but the doctrine of death; the Teacher; the Word of Islam. As Diallo has foreseen, the Teacher does not leave him even after death. From beyond the grave he reaches out to summon him, first creating Diallo's epiphany through the medium of the Fool, then through the same agency granting him absorption within the long-sought Ultimate. The quest-circle has been completed. The lesser pupil has preceded him in thought – thus the Chief of the Diallobe in a letter to Diallo on the death of the Teacher: 'The hour strikes when, if I had this choice at my disposal, I should choose to die.' It is the lesser concession that he later makes: 'Alas, I cannot even do as your old teacher did, lay aside that part of myself which belongs to men and leave it within their hands, while I withdraw.' But Samba Diallo *is* his designated successor. In the struggle of the secular need against the claims of mystic decadence the Teacher has the final say, and it is No. The Word emerges triumphant.

The contrast provided by Daniachew Worku in his attitude to his Ethiopian Christian material in *The Thirteenth Sun* (Heinemann, 1973) is very instructive. The work has many similarities to Hamidou Kane's concerns in *Ambiguous Adventure*. Its context is religion, and its setting is a pilgrimage. Death and corporeal corruption are eternal presences in this work also. The central character, or more accurately, the character around whom the action revolves, has embarked upon the pilgrimage to seek a cure. He dies in spite of priestly and other ministrations. In the process his son and daughter in their different ways achieve an accelerated maturity. Unlike Worku, there is no room in Hamidou Kane's

4   85

idealised portrayal of Diallobe reality for the slightest touch of irreverence. The figures are larger than life, they exist in a permanent refulgence of wisdom, purpose and spirituality. Their discourse is crafted with care, permitting no intrusion of trivia. Thought, deep reflection, sits constantly on their shoulders and casts a penumbra of remoteness around their smallest action. Even in the province of decadence, bones and corrupted flesh are given a sculptural dimension, old age and rheumatism in the weakening joints of the Sage merely provide occasion for experiencing a divine humour. Not so Dorku, for whom the language of death is the language of offal, flies and stench, just as his language of religion is the language also of fraud, charlatanism, gluttony and exploitation. The superstitions of Islamic religion are given a philosophical glow; Dorku melodramatises Ethiopian Christianity, allying its priesthood with the confused supernatural claims of a 'conjure-woman'. Worku's work presents no social vision however, and so does not really come within our frame of reference; but it does provide a conveniently divergent approach which emphasises the scale of dedication that has gone into Hamidou Kane's ideal projection, and reinforces the author's consciousness of choice.

When gods die – that is, fall to pieces – the carver is summoned and a new god comes to life. The old is discarded, left to rot in the bush and be eaten by termites. The new is invested with the powers of the old and may acquire new powers. In literature the writer aids the process of desuetude by acting as the termite or by ignoring the old deity and creating new ones. Sembene Ousmane, Yambo Oulouguem, Kwei Armah are among the leading practitioners of this method. But the process has been facilitated and complemented by a quite different school of iconoclasm, one which adopts the simple method of secularising the old deities. In African literature this is an organic step; the gods themselves, unlike the gods of Islam and Christianity are already prone to secularism; they cannot escape their history. The writer does little more than stretch that history into tangible and affective reality at whatever point of history he chooses to bring alive. Chinua Achebe's works are not strictly works that project a social vision, being primarily concerned with evocations of actuality at points where, to use Cabral's accurate expression, 'Africa was made to leave her history, her true history'. But Achebe (and later, Oulouguem) will serve as a bridge between the entrenchment of deities – indigenous and foreign – as mentors of social perspectives, and works of an assertive secular vision such as we encounter in Ousmane and others. The works of this latter group reveal the current trend in African writing, a trend which is likely to become more and more dominant as the intelligentsia of the continent seek ideological solutions that are truly divorced from the superstitious accretions of our alien encounters.

The secular nature of Achebe's *Arrow of God* (Doubleday, 1969) is actually poised on a very delicate ambiguity. Considerations of the authenticity of spiritual inspiration, or of manifestations which may be considered supernatural, or at the least, ominous coincidences, are given alternative (secular) explications in the casual reflections of members of his Igbo community, coloured as always by individual problems or positions taken in sectional confrontations. In short, coloured by their *humanity*. 'I have not said that Ezeulu is telling a lie with the name of Ulu or that he is not...' says Ogbuefi Ofoka. 'What we told him was to go and eat the yams and we would take the consequences.' The truth in that of course is that Achebe has himself raised the question. The unthinkable 'lie' has been rendered elastic in definition: what, in spiritual terms, is a lie? In the realms of psychological motivations knowledge of divine will loses its absolute affirmation. Why, in this connection, are we made to follow the priest into the shrine of Ulu, experience its macabre, if not its numinous power, but be robbed of the process of communication between priest and deity? The stylistic method to which we have been accustomed has until now, by contrast, been one of iteration – even of monotonous detail. A suggestion which proffers itself – that Achebe is drawn towards the preservation of the mystery of Ulu – proves unsatisfactory, as precedents to the contrary have been set throughout this work. The history of Ulu itself has robbed it even of the awe and reverence due to the autochthonous; Ulu the god proves less mysterious than the egwugwu, those mere ancestral spirits of the clan, and even they have been robed and disrobed before our gaze. No, an opportunity has been missed (and we must suspect deliberately so) to transmit even a fraction of the immanence of the deity, and the power of his priest to divine his will. The confrontation between god and priest is channelled off harmlessly through a prophetic glimpse of the god's own fate:

> As Ezeulu cast his string of cowries the bell of
> Oduche's people [the Christians' bell that is] began
> to ring. For one brief moment Ezeulu was distracted
> by its sad, measured monotone and thought how
> strange it was that it should sound so near – much
> nearer than it did in his compound. (p. 240)

The priest calls upon his deity but is answered by the bells of the Christian church. And afterwards, nothing but the laconic announcement that his consultation with his deity has produced no results.

The struggle among the gods has been placed squarely in the province of the political, and although the spiritual and the mysterious are never absent or invalidated – certainly the affective or responsive in the lives of the community is constantly used to reinforce this dimension of reality – yet the strongest arguments in favour of a divine factor in the life of Umuaro is deliberately subverted by impure associations insinuated through the manipulations of language, contradicting situations, or the preponderant claims of a secular wisdom. 'The gods sometimes use us as a whip' declares the priest of Ulu, boldly recreating his person as an extension, not so much of the gods, as of the principle of vengeance. But whose vengeance? After this, the indictment language of the kolanut which impiously remains unbroken to Ulu, the language of the silence of Umuaro in the face of provocation seems plaintive. And, as the elders of Umuaro point out, even Ulu has his price – it only remained for his priest to name it. The power of Ezeulu (and of Ulu by implication) to punish Winterbottom is never indisputably proposed. We know of Winterbottom's annual rendezvous with tropical fever; we know also that a predecessor of his had been carried away with the affliction. Nwodika, converted to Ezeulu's cause, hardly helps matters (in the reader's proportioning of forces that is) by feigning an illness of short duration, then pronouncing that this was no less than the work of Ezeulu, intended as a warning. The episode is suggestive of parallel practices. Ulu may have broken his priest, but Achebe laid fissures in his spiritual mould a long time before.

Ezeulu's own secular philosophy compounds the ambiguity. Join them (the Christians), he says to his son Oduche, and learn their ways, be my eyes and ears among them. One can hardly blame the arrogant *nouveau riche,* Nwaka, for turning this dangerous strategy against its practitioner. This was not, after all, a practised political intriguer but an impressionable youth. In his conversation with Nkubue, Ezeulu speaks in terms of sacrifice; does this mean he was fully reconciled to the inevitable, the thorough assimilation of his own son into the Christian faith?

'Who was Ezeulu to tell his deity how to fight the jealous cult of the sacred python?' This reprimand was the summation of the priest's inspired dialogue with Ulu and it led, naturally, into dangerous byways, not all of which he could even then perceive. If he had taken the argument further, re-examining his past action in the light of Ulu's avowed competence in the matter of defending his pre-eminence, he might have asked with equal validity: Who was Ezeulu to tell his deity how to fight the jealous cult of the Christian intruders? Indeed, he might have asked that question at the time of his decision to 'sacrifice' Oduche and not confine himself later within an untenable paradox. Ezeulu's failure to do this led him into rationally extended byways that even bordered upon religious treachery. If Oduche's minor act of sacrilege – boxing up the royal python – could be seen by Ezeulu as a possible device of the god Ulu, then we can only conclude that the deity was unwittingly digging his own grave. This was using the Christian rock to crush a housefly, a miscalculation which takes on even more self-destructive proportions if one accepts Ezeulu's speculations that Ulu's hand must be seen also in his (Ezeulu's) individual persecution by the white man; it resulted in his increased stature in Umuaro and enabled him to deal more effectively with the rival cult. To survive this factional threat, it would seem that the priest of Ulu *needed* the white man and his religion. Since we are left in no doubt at all that the priest of Ulu was shrewd, noble and motivated always by strong ethical considerations (witness his testimony against his own village in the land-dispute with Okperi) the plane of vision upon which his decisions are taken appears constantly to be a rationalised, even pragmatic plane. It is not an *inspired* plane of vision. In the carefully guided narration, we find more inspired moments in the eg-wugwu carrier than in the priest of Umuaro's leading deity.

Yet this priest aspires to no less than cosmic control.
The six villages, as a result of an unfruitful consultation,
would be locked in the old year for two moons longer.
The grandeur of this challenge is only mildly tempered
by the specious calculating game of numbers upon which
it rests – the fact that there are three yams left instead
of one. Again we encounter the priest's dogged seculari-
sation of the profoundly mystical. The supererogation
of Umuaro's elders pales beside his own: '*Umuaro is now
asking you to go and eat those remaining yams today and
name the day of the next harvest. . . I said go and eat
those yams today, not tomorrow; and if Ulu says we have
committed an abomination let it be on the heads of the
ten of us here. You will be free because we have set you
to it. . .*' (pp. 237–8). It is true that we have already been
subtly introduced to the innate transformation of the
thirteen yams, we have watched the Chief Priest at his
ritualistic meal on the appearance of the new moon and
understand him when he complains to the elders of
Umuaro that to eat one yam more than is prescribed is
to eat death. But we know Ezeulu is not afraid of death
– and death in Achebe's world is not simply the curtailing
of existence, but may embrace a more terrible loss of the
self. In short, Ezeulu is not afraid of self-sacrifice, whatever that may entail. It is therefore ironic that it is the
priest who deals in secular logic while the leaders suggest
spiritual remedies. 'I only call a new festival when there
is only one yam left,' he persists. 'Today I have three
yams and so I know that the time has not come.' And
it is for his visitors to suggest a recourse to the god, to
demand the price of appeasement. It is they who are
prepared 'to eat death' if the demand they make of their
priest proves to be abomination.

To the priest of Ulu, however, belongs the last word.
What he aims at, no less, is to lock the village in the old
year, and for no less than two moons. Its implications are
cosmic; the priest seeks to dislocate the perennial cycle

of Nature. The social and economic aspects recede into the background: planting and harvesting, festivals, rites and celebrations, all with their own season-related calendar. Perhaps it is the enormity of the idea that makes Achebe treat this hubristic conception in so skimpy a fashion. One short paragraph, one concession to an 'alarm as had not been known in Umuaro in living memory' and we are diverted firmly and definitively to the domestic squabbles that result from Ezeulu's action. There is a genuine feeling of being cheated, and this can be attributed to Achebe's own ambiguous stance. Ulu is kept unaware of, or at least is not made to participate in, the framing of this apocalyptic event. Obika's death is too perfunctory a divine reply, if indeed that is what it is, and the comment of the rival cult of Idemili: 'This should teach him how far he could dare next time' is too banal and jaundiced to match the conceptual scale of the cause itself. Event in literature is experienced according to its scale of treatment.

In Achebe's work, the gods are made an expression of the political unity (and disunity) of the people. Their history or measure (or both) testifies to their subjection to secular consciousness. However generously the element of the inexplicable is introduced into the lives of a community it is not possible, ultimately, for the gods to overcome their beginnings. The deity Ulu came into being as a result of a security decision, an expression of the survivalist will of the human community. It did not matter that a new political entity, Umuaro, also came into being as a result of this: 'how could such a people disregard the god who founded their town and protected it?' muses his priest. They could, because although a new existence was brought into being through the agency of the god, it was a purely political existence, not for instance a new conception or relationship of being. The will of this creative relationship remained with the human side of the partnership.

The lesser deities fare even worse. The festival of the New Yam was

> the one public appearance these smaller gods were
> allowed in the year. They rode into the market
> place on the heads or shoulders of their custodians,
> danced round and then stood side by side at the
> entrance to the shrine of Ulu. Some of them
> would be very old, nearing the time when their
> power would be transferred to new carvings and
> they would be cast aside; and some would have been
> made only the other day...Perhaps this year one
> or two more would disappear, following the men
> who made them in their own image and departed
> long ago. (pp. 231–2)

The passage sings the dirge, not merely of the gods of Umuaro but of godhood itself. It is not a sad sound, however, since it invests man and community with the 'life-force' of the gods. The life-force is not destroyed. Indeed Achebe suggests a residual feeling of immanence in the human unit. But the creator and custodian of the god is made man, not vice versa, and it is against this subtly established background that the personality of Ezeulu is cast. What comes through then, finally, of this personality who was himself an embodiment of the vital forces of Umuaro?

We can examine this question firstly from an external viewpoint – his relationship, as experienced in himself, with Winterbottom. We are friends, he remarks of Winterbottom, and his friendship is meant in an ethical sense – friendship of a man who recognises truth and acknowledges the man who speaks it. But that recognition of friendship predicates a basis of equality: Winterbottom, in Ezeulu's mind, should know better than to summon peremptorily the Chief Priest of Ulu. Next, Winterbottom should know better than to attempt to make the

Chief of Ulu his own instrument. We may also consider whether Ezeulu's rejection of the white man's offer of chieftaincy is based on a conflict between secular and spiritual loyalties: there is no evidence of such a conflict. 'Tell the white man that Ezeulu will not be anybody's chief, except Ulu.' This tells us nothing, except we first understand how Ezeulu sees Ulu in relation to himself. We can recapitulate how. The evidence suggests that the priest spurns Winterbottom on socio-political grounds, that is, as the representative of the community of Umuaro, the ethical standard-bearer and repository of the social will. For this proud priest, it becomes a contradiction of his functions to accept a mandate from a rival polity. Ulu is fused, in Ezeulu's dealing with Winterbottom, with Umuaro. '...Ezeulu will not be anybody's chief except Ulu.' Can we really, from the presentation so far of Ulu and his priest, read Ezeulu's mind and understand him as saying, 'I cannot serve God and Man'? It does not appear so. All that has preceded this confrontation negates such an interpretation. Throughout Ezeulu's incarceration we see Ulu merely as the instrument of the priest's will. Achebe, deliberately or not, avoids any spiritual dimensions in the priest's experience of exile. Considerations of functions, yes, and even these (including his vision) are elaborations of the internecine politics. That, in his vision, he is actually spat upon and called the 'priest of a dead god' does not trigger off in him any spiritual alarm; only regrets that he has, in actuality, temporarily lost the status of Chief Priest. Achebe keeps all the implications of exile firmly in the secular world, reducing them even further with an infusion of one domestic drama after another. This is the immediate context provided for us by the sound of Ezeulu's response to the white man's offer. And his stature – the apprehension of his dignity among his countrymen – is rooted in his social being, not in a religious priesthood. The 'spirit half' of Ezeulu as occasionally

stressed by his friend Akuebue appears constantly repressed at the high points of his drama.

In the final pages however, we come up against a
difficulty. Ezeulu's lamentations are phrased in the pietist
language of god-abandonment, not as protests against
such abstractions as Fate or Destiny, nor even as acknowledgement of the possibility that he, who has warned
so many against such an error, had finally challenged his
personal *chi*. It is the same language as we have encountered in Kane except for a difference in the individual's
mode of experience – a temperamental difference – and
the authors' metaphors of expression. 'Why, he asked
himself again and again, why had Ulu chosen to deal thus
with him, to strike him down and cover him with mud?'
Taken together with Ezeulu's earlier dialogue with Ulu
(as he toyed with the idea of relenting in his scheme to
punish the people of Umuaro), this constitutes the strongest expression yet of Ulu as a distinct active Consciousness. The leaders of Umuaro reinforce it. 'To them the
issue was simple. Their god had taken sides with them
against their headstrong and ambitious priest and thus
upheld the wisdom of their ancestors...' But Achebe is
not for that reason about to give the last word to the god.
Even here, the god is made to serve the ends of the
ancestors, the clan, the people. And there are implications in this judgement for the god himself, for have we
not already in this narrative encountered gods who were
destined for a finale not dissimilar to that of the priest?
We have learnt already how the people of Aninta dealt
with their deity when he failed them: carried him to the
boundary between them and their neighbours and set
fire to him. In emphasising that Ulu had merely upheld
the communal will, an element of the god's own precarious existence is under-scored. The god can initiate
nothing, it seems; his role is that of an executor of
decisions already taken, or affirmer of secular ethos. And
as it happens, while Ulu may have interpreted correctly

the wishes of the majority of Umuaro, he has failed to divine the historic factors at work. His timing is so tactless that be brings disaster on himself, handing over a rich social harvest from Umuaro to the proselytising Christians. We are left with a hanging prediction that Ulu has set his course for the exact fate of the god of Aninta, figuratively at least. Ezeulu, not Ulu, is cast as the summation of the life-force of Umuaro; without him, the god is reduced to an empty shell.

4

Ideology and the social vision (2): The secular ideal

A certain Lothrop Stoddard prophesied as follows (the year was 1920):

> Certainly, all white men, whether professing christians or not, should welcome the success of missionary efforts in Africa. The degrading fetishism and demonology which sum up the native pagan cults cannot stand, and all Negroes will some day be either christians or moslems.[1]

Africa minus the Sahara North is still a very large continent, populated by myriad races and cultures. With its millions of inhabitants it must be the largest metaphysical vacuum ever conjured up for the purpose of racist propaganda. Mongo Beti is perhaps the most assiduous writer to have taken up the challenge of Mr Stoddard, dealing expertly and authentically with the claims of Christianity as a filler of spiritual holes. His weapon is a deceptive generosity which disguises, until the last moment, a destructive logic, incontestible in its consistent exposition of cause and effect. His priests are never complete villains but are revealed to be complete fools. Even where he has presented the representative of the Christian Church as a figure of inner doubts on the way to eventual enlightenment, it is only a refinement of Mongo Beti's delectable hypocrisy – his exactions will be doubly cruel and thorough. Thus, in *King Lazarus* the Rev. Father le Guen, stiff-necked to the last, merely loses

[1] Quoted in Charles DeGraft-Johnson, *The Rising Tide of Colour against White World Supremacy*, Chapman and Hall, London, 1926, p. 96.

his position and is left with the consolation of commiserating with himself as a victim of colonial administrative intrigues. The only reprisal from the victims of his spiritual assault is to witness the reversion of his prize convert to the joys of polygamy. The poor Christ of Bomba is an equally stubborn prelate. He is even more manic in his encounters with 'heathen' practices but by contrast, is revealed as a man tortured by increasing doubts. His inner reflections promise a conversion, some hope for the salvation of the man is awakened in the breast of the reader. But Mongo Beti is not about to redeem his gull. The ramifications of a venereal denouement cover the Father Superior with the stench of failure. Beti's thesis reads: the Church is, by its very nature (doctrine and practice), a contagion; Mongo Beti's expositions are masterly erosions of the Christian myth.

The virtues of Mongo Beti's works tempt detailed elaborations but he is strictly outside our frame of reference. His task is the demolition of pretenders to cultural and spiritual superiority, not a re-statement of the values of past or present in integrated perspectives of a future potential. This latter process need not be overt or didactic; it need only translate the inherent or stated viable values of a social situation into a contemporary or future outlook, engaging the reader's collaboration through sympathetic characters and value judgements operated by a contrasting habit of the mind. Iconoclasm by itself may embody a social vision, and the question is certainly raised by Oulouguem's uncompromising work, *Bound to Violence*.[2]

But first, a problem which cannot be honestly ignored. The charges of plagiarism in Oulouguem's work appear to be well substantiated; it would be futile to deny this. The literary question remains, however, whether or not we are confronted with an original contribution to

[2] Yambo Oulouguem, *Bound to Violence*, translated by Ralph Manheim, Secker & Warburg, London, 1971.

literature, in spite of the borrowings. The *drama* of the novel is original; this, I believe, has not been disputed. The stylistic 'griot' propulsive energy and the creative vision are unquestionably Ourouguem's. It has been claimed that the thematic structure has been borrowed also from a previous Prix Renaudot winner; by this I mean the disposition of theme into the transmitting media of events, place and temporal relations. I have not read the other work so this question is one which I cannot resolve. There are also moral and philosophical questions. The former can be resolved quite simply: it would have been preferable if Yambo Oulouguem had acknowledged his sources. The philosophical aspect concerns the principle of ownership of the written word. This was the line which I rather expected Oulouguem to adopt in his response to the charges, not from any interest in the results but in anticipation of a debate which, given the French penchant for speculative philosophy, would certainly have resulted in obscuring the original issues and left Oulouguem's readers to carry on regarding his work as literature, until given evidence to the contrary. Which is precisely what I propose to do.

The charge of plagiarism was, however, not the only reaction produced by the work. It is not surprising, given the nature of the political alliances which dominate the world at present, to find that the intelligentsia of the black world are in ideological disagreement over the question whether enforced cultural and political exocentricity, as a retarding factor in the authentic history and development of Black Africa, should be recognised as appertaining only to the European world. The existence of the school of thought which thinks *not* is our present concern, nor is its expression among African writers and intellectuals as new as is commonly supposed. Yambo Oulouguem unquestionably triggered off the critical alarm in the opposing school, but what he has done with his fictional re-creation of history is no more nor less than a Cheik Anta Diop or Chancellor Williams has done for decades in their several essays on African civilisation. The researches and findings of Diop, Williams, Frobenius and other historians and ethno-scientists made *Le Devoir de Violence* inevitable and salutary – Oulouguem's savage satire on Sh(F)robeniosology notwithstanding. The outcry of sections of black American militancy over this aspect of the book is simply misguided.

Le Devoir de Violence (I shall use the original in preference to the English version of the title) marks a studied repudiation of historic blinkers. It re-writes the chapter of Arab–Islamic colonisation of Black Africa, but moves beyond history and fiction to raise questions of the very structure of racial heritage. Accepted history is held against an exhumed reality; the resulting dialectic can only lead to a reassessment of contemporary society and its cultural equipment for racial advance. This intellectual dimension of the writing places it amongst the literature of prognostic enquiry, in spite of the negative approach. The question is implicitly assertive: if 'Negro art (and culture, history) found a patent of nobility in the folklore of mercantile intellectualism', what constituted the authentic nobility of Negro art? The tapestry of repudiation comes alive before our eyes, as if a light is played upon it, activating shadow after shadow with its blood-red illumination. A neutral, tight-lipped humour fitfully relieves the oppression, varying from the mordant and sardonic to cosmic belly-laughs; great passages of history are set in motion by a public split in the trousers of the great. The Bible, the Koran, the historic solemnity of the griot are reduced to the histrionics of wanton boys masquerading as humans. Oulouguem leaps frenetically from the cliché 'café au lait' joke to the sadistic guffaw with the lofty indifference of a ringmaster manipulating his whirl of freaks at the touch of a foot-pedal, halting long enough to treat his audience to a little perversion act, then moving on to the next exhibit. Is there a touch of self-hate in Oulouguem's 'dispassionate' recital? The intensity of contempt for the victims is clearly intended to reflect the alienation of the torturers from the concept of the victims as human, to reflect their religious–imperial justification for acts of barbarism, yet beneath this device lurks, one suspects, the discomfort of the author himself. The epithets are spat through gritted teeth; the antidote for victim-identification appears to be a deflective masochism – Oulouguem has been accused of an alienation technique; the opposite seems truer – such a level of inventive degradation suggests that Oulouguem is practising some form of literary magic for the purpose of self-inoculation.

Oulouguem has also carried the devaluation technique (through proximity and non-differentiation) to its conceivable limits. The method is invariably iconoclastic; nothing survives in it, not even love or (to keep our demands modest in a work of this nature) mutual physical attraction. Kassoumi's love for Tambira (both serfs) is not permitted to remain long in the natural order of things. Custom dictates that he resort to the burning of 'nail parings, three eyelashes, seven head hairs, seven pubic hairs etc., etc.' to sprinkle on the bride's nuptial viands; while for himself crushed lion-penises, cocks' testicles and goat sperm provide the fare. The obscenity of the seigneur's right of the first night prolongs the reductive cynicism of the event (the novel's first *human* event) by its own ceremonial burnings of 'incense, sublimate of camphor, aloes, Indian musk and amber' in a mockery of defloration. Slave and master are made to undergo these humiliations with complete equanimity; the law of the absurd and the obscene, narratively imposed until now, becomes fully sublimated in the first human realist portraiture. This is the first moment that the semblance of an individuated character (and contact) has emerged from the tapestry, but its function is merely to confirm and reinforce the pattern of the established norm; from here on, further human delineation will immerse each product of Nakem's history in the gory degradation of its past, and most deeply, our would-be central character, fruit of the obscene rites of the union of serfs – Raymond Spartacus Kassoumi.

In preparation for the summative European pilgrimage of the young Kassoumi, art, religion and cultural concepts are brought together in contemporary time for a final iconoclastic collision, elaborating Oulouguem's cynical observation noted earlier in the midst of mayhem: 'the blessed union of knowledge and morality is fragile'. Kassoumi's quest for knowledge (and liberation) is foredoomed; he will neither escape his Nakem past nor its present transposition to the 'Shrobeniusology' of distant Europe. The avenues of possible salvation through religion are firmly closed, even to the extent of assailing their modern defenders with that most lethal weapon, parody. For instance, the metempsychotic delirium of the wife-murderer Sankolo reads suspiciously like a sex-orgiastic parody of Hamidou Kane's transcendentalist apologia for Islamic spirituality. Recourse to an indigenous metaphysics, a 'cosmological religiosity' or 'inner landscape' has become impossible, because it is deprived of identity by the intellectual conmanship of Europe's anthropologists. The pathway in that direction is clotted up with the superficial debris of intellectual excavations. The Shrobenious invasion of Nakem is stretched to represent the tradition of falsification, coupled with a levelling down of the Aryan myth, the symbolic blonde beast brought to rut in the degenerate earth of black Nakem, naturally enough in the context of the highest quest conceivable to German civilisation – the quest for *Kultur*! But even as the concepts of Aryan self-reversal are mouthed, ostensibly to compensate for the long heresy of Eurocentric belittlement of black Africa, they are brought flatly down within sordid motivations – entrepreneurial greed and opportunism even in the service of Kultur! The idea that the revolutionary potential of Nakem's serfdom will approach this source for intellectual sustenance compounds the sham. Study for young Kassoumi has become a 'fanatical cult', the 'instrument of his liberation'. But the quality of all possible knowledge is falsified in advance; worse, the foundation of his elevation, his mother's sordid sacrifice, hangs over any eventual achievement like a miasma. Oulouguem excels himself: not only does the mother prostitute herself to the sorcerer for her sons' success, she is subsequently raped by Saif's two gorillas then murdered (or commits suicide) in the slaves' latrine, up to the neck in excrement. Kassoumi's father lovingly sucks the worms from her nostrils!

How ironic that the novel's only episode of consciously rendered affectionate relationship should be homosexual, and yet how appropriate to Oulouguem's misanthropic vision! It raises questions, certainly. The tender narrative of Raymond Spartacus' affair with the Strasbourgois, Lambert, is such a drastic departure from the rest of the narrative, containing so little of the earlier brutality or cynical undermining, that it reads like a heightened James Baldwin. It is not only tender, it is *sympathetic* and sincere despite the occasions when the author, recalled to himself, appears to feel obliged to liken Kassoumi's love to that of a whipped dog, or acknowledges in Lambert an 'obscure desire to get even, to avenge himself, to wound his nigger'. Such insertions are both rare and even self-conscious, betraying a suspicious desire to complicate, to keep some level of dialectic tension going at all costs by exploiting the racial context. The mercenary calculation of Raymond Spartacus at the start is made ambivalent even in the very first night of copulation. Nothing wrong with that, but what we encounter is not lust, in keeping with Nakem's history of pederasty, sodomy, sexual sadism, etc., but tenderness.

Yet nothing till now has suggested Kassoumi's homosexual leanings. The morning request for payment for his
services sounds pathetic rather than commercial, and of
course he soon graduates to the status of a kept 'mistress'
in what is clearly no longer a commercial arrangement
but one of love. Long after Spartacus has ceased to need
Lambert financially, the affair is continued by both. The
significance of this episode is certainly elusive, since its
treatment removes it from the pale of suggestive criticism
or subjective contempt either of European decadence or
of the individuals. Such solemn cadences, extolling the
anal salvation of the lonely in the inhuman and indifferent society of Europe belong to the fictional prose
of Baldwin and Genêt, and cannot be integrated into
the mould of iconoclastic literature. Neither, incidentally, can the Victorian melodrama of brother-beds-
sister-in-brothel fable. This reads at first like an
attempted parody, but it then becomes the instrument
of crucial relevations of homeland for Spartacus (and a
further confirmation of his whipped character). The
extension of the melodrama into the neurotic reality of
the milieu – the razor blade in the bidet soap which ends
Kadidia's life a bare week later – only mildly restores the
earlier consistency, being a predictable extension of the
violent destiny of the Nakemians. But then, a short while
later, the incongruously tender homosexual interlude!

If there is any doubt that *Le Devoir de Violence* owes
much in its conception to a desire to counter the Islamic
apologia of Hamidou Kane, the duplication of the hero's
pilgrimage to Europe dispels much of it and the final
duet of the Bishop and the Saif, a confrontation in the
idiom of grim political exegesis which corresponds to
Hamidou Kane's mystic exegesis of death, removes the
last of it. But the reaches of *Le Devoir de Violence* are
far wider; the work does not specifically address itself to
the Islamic myth. It is a fiercely partisan book on behalf
of an immense historic vacuum, the vacuum this time

being Oulouguem's creation, not Stoddard's. And the charge of (unlocated) racism is departicularised by the author's uniform manipulation of the rhetorical style of the legendary heroes and their associative civilisations: Judaic, medieval, Arab–Islamic, Christian–European. The neat juxtaposition of incongruous prayers and pietistic lore with events of cunning, duplicity and barbarism may seem an obvious literary device but, since the characters themselves appear perfectly at home in this tradition of florid diplomacy (French, Arabic, and so on) the author's organising hand is hardly felt. Statesmanship and strategies are snared and rendered indistinguishable from the mere rhodomontade of the discourse of duplicity, a medieval variant of Newspeak. A culture which has claimed indigenous antiquity in such parts of Africa as have submitted to its undeniable attractions is confidently proven to be imperialist; worse, it is demonstrated to be essentially hostile and negative to the indigenous culture. As a purely sociological event, such a work was bound to create violent passions. Reinterpretations of history or contemporary reality for the purpose of racial self-retrieval do generate extremes of emotion, most of all among claimants to intellectual objectivity. Oulouguem's verdict is a painful one – a sanguinary account of the principal rival to the Christian mission in Africa cannot be anything but provocative. Oulouguem pronounces the Moslem incursion into black Africa to be corrupt, vicious, decadent, elitist and insensitive. At the least such a work functions as a wide swab in the deck-clearing operation for the commencement of racial retrieval. The thoroughness of its approach – total and uncompromising rejection – can only lead to the question already posed: what was the authentic genius of the African world before the destructive alien intrusion? And the question can today be confidently asked, backed as it is is by findings from the labour of ethnoscientists. Stoddard's thesis is predictably exposed as fallacious; the alternative candidate for stuffing up the cultural black hole of the continent is yet another rubble-maker of cultural edifices.

It is true that Oulouguem takes no interest in present-ing to the reader the values destroyed in this process. The positive does not engage his re-creative attention, and what glimpse we obtain of the indigenous reality is presented within the undifferentiated context of the oppressed and the oppressor, the feudal overlord and slave – undifferentiated, that is, from the later political relations of Arab and European colonialism. Oulouguem speaks indeed of a 'black colonialism'.[3] The premise for this expression is suspect, and it has affected Oulou-guem's concepts of the pre-colonial reality of African society. A social condition in which Semites (though black and pre-Islamic) are overlords and negro-Africans the slaves still leaves the basic curiosity about black historic reality unsatisfied. Not until Ayi Kwei Armah's *Two Thousand Seasons* (East African Publishing House, 1973) is this aspect attempted; but even there its validity is not predicated on objective truths so much as on the fulfil-ment of one of the social functions of literature: the visionary reconstruction of the past for the purposes of a social direction. In Armah's work, there is no ambiva-lence of intent, nor of historic reconstruction.

The Eurocentric burden of black Africa attains com-plete identification, in Armah's work, with Arab–Islamic colonialism. Arab slavers are referred to as *white* men, not only in the narrative, but more importantly as the characteristic definition by those Africans whose subju-gation and liberation-struggle make up the story. Armah's images reinforce this general perspective on the Arab presence: the employment of the white desert as symbol of an insatiable suction on life, yielding in return only bones and emptiness, this white image of death is married with the other predatory whiteness: white mag-

[3] Interview published in JONALA 9/10.

gots swarming from over the seas, the European slavers. The theologies of both groups of intruders are interpreted through parallel life-denying metaphors, both cultures are equated with systems to which human depravity is not only natural but essential. The anti-humanism of the mass enslavement of other beings is not even left to speak for itself; Armah is anxious that the theological collaboration in this orgy of bestialisation is not missed. As if in stung response to Lothrop Stoddard, Armah declares:

> We have not found that lying trick to our taste, the
> trick of making up sure knowledge of things
> possible to think of, things possible to wonder about
> but impossible to know in any such ultimate way.
> We are not stunted in spirit, we are not Europeans,
> we are not christians that we should invent fables a
> child would laugh at and harden our eyes to preach
> them daylight and night as truth. We are not so
> warped in soul, we are not Arabs, we are not
> muslims to fabricate a desert god chanting madness
> in the wilderness, and call our creature creator.
> That is not our way. (*Two Thousand Seasons,* p. 4)

Once again we must attempt to place this unusual vehemence against its full background. The quest for and the consequent assertion of the black cultural psyche began as a result of the deliberate propagation of untruths by others, both for racist motives and to disguise their incapacity to penetrate the complex verities of black existence. Cheikh Anta Diop and Chancellor Williams go so far as to accuse their European counterparts not only of a deliberate falsification of history (as interpreted), but of the suppression and falsification of historic evidence. Diop's re-interpretation of the evidence for the history of civilisation goes so far as to question the origin of European and Northern culture and replace it in the South, in the Negro cradle. (Diop simplifies the division of the races into two – the Southern, black; and the Northern, white, Arab or European.) The sentient individual for his own part must be constantly recollected as one who has experienced histories which he is aware are not his own, and whose sense of identity is unstable, consisting in effect of the process of coming to terms with the history of others in conflict with his own repressed cultural and ethnic being. It is an active sense of identity; and where the ethno-scientist stops is where the re-creative energy takes over: both activities are aspects of and complement each other. The reverse, it must be remembered, is also true. The Eurocentric ethnologist has been complemented for centuries by European literature from Elizabethan imagination to the Rider Haggards and the Kiplings, not to mention the image-manufacturers of Euro-American cinema. It has not all been a crude and obvious misrepresentation; not only has some of it been well-intended but some has actually originated from among black scholars and writers. Thus, Bolaji Idowu in his otherwise excellent work, *Olodumare: God in Yoruba Belief* (Longman, 1962) makes a point of proving that the Yoruba do believe in a Supreme Deity, with this dominating inference – that this constitutes proof of the high stage of development of the Yoruba people. Such a criterion of development is, need one add, entirely Eurocentric.

The proliferation of such myths, and their implicit acceptance even today on the African continent must be seen and understood as the background to the works under discussion. Failure to see the process of racial retrieval in one comprehensive whole, to see the process of anti-colonialism as one which ends with far greater ramifications for society *in depth* than the rejection of *one* self-assertive set of values, suggests a lack of faith in, or a half-hearted attempt to re-discover and re-examine the matrix of society that preceded the violent distortions. A rejection of the Eurocentric incubus which has preoccupied African creative writing almost exclusively for half a century cannot fail, in an intelligent people, to answer more questions than it began by posing. Political revolutions of a race-retrieving nature such as the overthrow of the Sultanate autocracy in Zanzibar by an indigenous African nationalist movement have consequences far beyond those of similar violent changes in political authority in other areas. That the Afro-Shirazi Party under Sheik Karume later became as suspiciously repressive as the alien imperialism it overthrew is another matter entirely, an unfortunate fact of political change which is not confined to Africa. What really concerns us here is that political events such as those which took place in Zanzibar or the Sudan are components of the same mould of thought and expression as the literature of the now restive modern product of centuries of alien historic impositions. The long ignominious silence of African leaders over the now resolved Anyanya insurrection in the Sudan is, alas, the misleading yardstick by which the majority judge the truth of such expressions of the authentic will to identity. Missing always is that temper of comprehension which recognises in the various adaptive modes of expression aspects of the same crucial struggle for a re-statement of self and society. Cheikh Anta Diop, Sheikh Karume, Oulouguem, Ayi Kwei Armah, Anyanya? A puzzled headshake signifying – No Connection. But how can the intellectual be blamed when national leaders have trivialised the essential with catch-all diversionary slogans such as 'authenticité'! Ayi Akwei Armah does not neglect to portray the opportunistic existence of such 'kings' in his contribution to the search for a social direction.

It is Armah's attention to such critical details as the false prophets of retrieval that rescues the work from its less defensible excesses. For when all the excuses have been made and the *historic inevitability* of this genre of writing fully accepted, there still remains a feeling of discomfort over the actual language of confrontation and the dramatic devices in which the victims of the author's ire are trapped. In contrast to Oulouguem, however, Armah's work is intensely committed to the substitution of another view of *active* history, with re-creating humanistic perspectives as inspirational alternatives to existing society. His vision consciously conforms to no inherited or imposed religious doctrine and attendant ethics, frees itself of borrowed philosophies in its search for a unifying, harmonising ideal for a distinctive human-ity. Because it is not possible to suspend the awareness of these integrated goals in the narrative, the recession of the idiom of humanism becomes particularly oppres-sive on occasion. There is a gleefulness, a reckless ascend-ancy of the vengeance motif in passages such as these:

> Came a Rhamadan, the predators' season of hypocritical self-denial. Followed the time they call the Idd, time of the new moon of their new year. After a month of public piety and abstention the predators again threw themselves into their accustomed orgies of food, of drugs and of sex. Of these orgies we remember the greatest, and for those particular predators the last...(*Two Thousand Seasons*, p. 31)

> Hussein, twin brother of Hassan the Syphilitic. Hussein had long since given up the attempt to find a way for his phallus into any woman's genitals. His tongue was always his truest pathfinder. So after moving with the others in the forgetfulness of a momentary genital enthusiasm he had returned to eating buttered dates into his bursting paunch, buttered dates mined from three women's holes in turn. By the third round the circuit was making Hussein dizzy. The third woman therefore held Hussein's head in a tender caress. The second in a gesture full of love stuck a smooth, solid,

well-honed knife into Hussein's neck, in a soft space between the cowries of his spine. The first woman stroked the disjointed head with affection, pressing it firmly down so the first hoarse cry from the throat came out a muffled sound of happy lechery. Then the first woman raised the head gently, to give the warm blood way in its quiet flowing from the predator's open mouth...(p. 34)

This is how Hassan died: at the height of his oblivious joy a seventh woman unknown to him but known to the other six brought a horn holed at its small end as well as the large, and inserted the small end into the Arab's rectum. Hassan was overjoyed. A torrent of thanks and praises was pouring out of his mouth, directed toward the slaveowner benefactor god who had so thoughtfully provided such exquisite means to the completion of his pleasure when he felt something extra reach the lining of his rectum. It was honey, mixed with lamp oil, the mixture heated past boiling. Hassan's unforeseen benefactress poured an overflowing measure of the sweet liquid into his arse. (p. 38)

In the depravities of the Arab invaders of Africa, in the horrendous means of eliminating which the author devises for them, evolving these from their favourite perversions in a kind of sexual justice, the humane sensibility tends to recoil a little. Their brothers, the white maggots from over the seas, fare no better. The one Armah calls the predators, the other, destroyers; both predatory birds are decked in the same feathers. Through the eyes of the indigenes, the askaris, the harem guards, the middlemen, the fugitives, we encounter all aliens as inhuman exploiters only; there is no redeeming grace, no event is permitted to establish the exception.

In spite of this, *Two Thousand Seasons* is not a racist

tract; the central theme is far too positive and dedicated and its ferocious onslaught on alien contamination soon falls into place as a preparatory exercise for the liberation of the mind. A clean receptive mind is a prerequisite for its ideological message, and there is no question that this work is designed for the particular audience of Armah's own race. What he offers them now is 'the way', 'our way'. True, beyond the method of contrasts, beyond the utilisation of fertility and regeneration in contrast with the barren insatiability of the desert, beyond its summation in the oft-recurring word 'reciprocity' and its attributive 'connectedness', the Way is not very distinctly specified. But we learn that it is the way of life while others are the way of death. Nor is the goal of the Way attainable by mere passive understanding; it is mandated upon the destruction for all time of the agencies of opposition. This is the primary mission. The bare cleared earth, a restored, receptive virginity, is in conformity with Armah's own progressive device. Indeed, Armah appears to have undertaken this preliminary literary destruction of the identified opposition as a parallel activity to the novel's schematism. But except for the occasional utterances of its seers – the elderly Isanusi and Adewa the virgin mystic – the Way remains a hazy and undefined ideology; it is the action that defines it, and the guiding principles debated by the protagonists.

Progressively, the blotted-out areas of ethical harmony, long obliterated by the impositions of alien structures, are filled out. Ayi Kwei Armah asserts a past whose social philosophy was a natural egalitarianism, unravelling events which produced later accretions of the materialist ethic in order to reinforce the unnaturalness, the abnormality of the latter. The actions of his protagonists are aimed at the retrieval of that past, but again Armah insists that this past is not a nostalgic or sentimental one. It is presented as a state embodying a rational ideal. Armah goes even farther; actions and motivations are deliberately contrived to place such longings (for a nostalgic past) in a context of betrayal of the larger aim; as self-delusion, self-destruction and general mindlessness. In the same way as the materialist retrogression of the modern African polity is an implied target of the author's savage attack, so also is the romanticism of Negritude assailed in associative portrayals.

The members of an initiation group betrayed to a white (European) slaver by their own king have freed themselves from the boat while it is still in coastal waters. They escape, take to the forest and engage in guerilla warfare against the 'destroyers'. In the process they also free other groups who are then offered the choice of returning to their homes or joining with their rescuers in the liberation struggle. Armah's warning is that their real enemy, the eternal middlemen among their own kind, are merely waiting to sell them off again. Those who fail to recognise this reality encounter their fate, as predicted. The physical action becomes a parable for the crippling nostalgia which drags society back into an unreal past. It is one of the strongest themes of the book. And such hankerings are contrasted with a concerted, purposed preparation for a return to Anoa, the original home of the fugitive band; the physical road to Anoa is thus rendered separate from the ideological road. Monarchy is quietly undermined by its historical reconstruction: the past of kings is not the real past; the kings stand revealed as part of the historical rupture, stooges brought into existence through the agency of the incoming marauders who needed puppet figures of arbitrary authority to bargain with for slaves and trade monopolies, mercenaries who could be armed and supported and set upon neighbouring peoples and their own subjects alike. The universally applicable ideal is constantly verified by recourse to such known historic instances. The frame of absurdity is used to shatter anti-social notions, such as the sanctity of property:

> For the first time among us one man tried to turn
> the land into something cut apart and owned. It was
> asked what next the greedy would think to own –
> the air? (p. 100)

For the modern African who has watched the principle
of communal land-ownership crumble before the rapac-
ious march of development monopoly, the process
seems after all reversible. But Armah is nothing if not
realistic:

> An unknown avenger sent him hurrying to face the
> wrath of his ancestors, but that was not the end of
> the greed of kings. (pp. 100–1)

There are of course serious weaknesses in the book.
The long seer-run overture occasionally creaks, and
Armah's prose style appears unequal to the task of
capturing action and rendering it totally convincing. This
weakness often tends to make the book read like an
adventure story. But his protagonists remain convincing
visionaries of society, mostly because Armah makes no
concessions in this unusual book, not even to the rhetoric
of revolution to which lesser writers so readily succumb.
Its vision is secular and humane, despising alike the
flatulence of religious piety and its proselytising aggres-
siveness, insisting on a strict selectivity from the past in
the designing of the future. There is evident impatience
with the state of racial enervation which is Armah's
interpretation of the unquestioning submission to imposed history, religion and culture and the consequent
exteriorised self-definition. Most remarkable of all in a
book which is hardly squeamish in its depiction of
violence, is Armah's insistence on a revolutionary integrity, a refusal to be trapped into promoting the increasingly fashionable rhetoric of violence for its own
sake. The foundation of this physical caution is laid in
the matrix of a philosophy that he elicits from a now

familiarised past and makes a condition for a tenable future. This humanistic recourse to proportion and the principle of totalism in the book's summation rationalises the nature of struggle. Violence, death, destruction and sacrifice are acceptable, but the part, the motion or the act cannot be elevated above the whole:

> We do not utter praise of arms. The praise of arms is the praise of things, and what shall we call the soul crawling so low, soul so hollow it finds fulfilment in the praising of mere things? It is not things we praise in our utterance, not arms we praise but the living relationship itself of those united in the use of all things against the white sway of death, for creation's life... Whatever thing, whatever relationship, whatever consciousness takes us along paths closer to our way, whatever goes against the white destroyers' empire, that thing is beautiful, that relationship only is truthful, that consciousness alone has satisfaction for the still living mind. (p. 320)

The secular vision in African creative writing is particularly aggressive wherever it combines the re-creation of a pre-colonial African world-view with eliciting its transposable elements into a modern potential. The process may be explicit, as in Armah's *Two Thousand Seasons,* or, as in Sembene, may rely on the reader's capacity for projection. The shared knowledge of what now exists and the prior assumption of a readership subjectively attuned to the significations of posed comparisons is part of the armoury of the novel which, depending on the moralities of the conflicts and events, does away with the need for utopian presentations. Assuming an unsympathetic readership, it remains a threat, a potent one, because its justifying paradigm has been woven from the authentic heritage of that society. The greater the realism, the more dangerous it appears to be: when, as in Sembene, the subject is a recent historic actuality, the author can expect classification as a security risk. Sometimes, because of the static appearance of the novel's social moralities, it is dismissed as harmless – Armah's earlier work *The Beautyful Ones are Not Yet Born* (Heinemann, 1969) may be placed in this category. Despite its criticism of social values and their pursuit at a particularly delicate period of his country's post-colonial history, its excoriation of internal social corruption, because expanded into nearly metaphysical dimensions may, beyond banal protests at such 'unflattering portraits' of a young nation, awaken no anxiety in the establishment such as might arise from a directly contradicting social vision. The vision is there nevertheless, and is perhaps more subtly subversive than in his latter explicit work, *Two Thousand Seasons.* The vision of *The Beautyful Ones* is perhaps no more than an aspiration, a pious hope symbolised in that final image of the novel – 'a single flower, solitary, unexplainable, very beautiful' in the centre of the inscription on the back of a mammy-waggon which reads: THE BEAUTYFUL ONES ARE NOT YET BORN. This pessimistic suggestion bears the possibility of its own hopeful contradiction, an accurate summation of society only too well understood by Armah and expressed in the main action of the book through the solitary, beleaguered representative of moral possibilities, the central character (and his friend, the Teacher). There is also the hopeful portent inherent in the physical and moral collapse of the 'unbeautyful' ones as history revenges itself on them. Without miring ourselves in Armah's appropriately scatological metaphor, there is a readiness of association which transfers the image of the flower to an excremental genesis, personalising its symbolism in the character of the unnamed hero.

After that work Ayi Kwei Armah had to attempt to give birth to the 'beautyful' in the creative progression of *Two Thousand Seasons.* Ousmane Sembene performs a similar midwife role in his *God's Bits of Wood* (Heinemann, 1970), a powerful reconstruction of a strike by African railway workers in 1947. It is a work which reaches beyond mere narrative in its meticulous delineation of human strengths and weaknesses, heroism and communal solidarity, and it attains epic levels. As with all good epics, humanity is re-created. The social community acquires archetypal dimensions and heroes become deities. Even Penda the prostitute is apotheosised.

The remote, enigmatic Bakayako is a Promethean creation, a replacement for outworn deities who have the misfortune to lose their relevance in a colonial world. Amoral in the mundane sense of the word, Bakayako appears to be sculpted out of pure intellect and omniscience. Not merely because the established Islamic Voice in the community is shown to be treacherous and reactionary but because Bakayako is portrayed as understanding and controlling the future (or at least the path towards it) he supersedes all existing moral authority and forges, through his inflexible will, the unique community of the Railway Line into a force that robs the other deity, the Colonial Super-reality, of its power. Of course the portraiture of Bakayoko is somewhat romanticised – necessarily so. He is a man of mystery, irresistible to women and dominating to all. To the precocious child Ad'jibid'ji he is perfection, manifestly superior to all humanity around him. And he represents a gifted world that she only vaguely feels. He tends to the poetic, and his perception of the world takes from his own innate grandeur: 'She looks like the bronze masks of a goddess of Ife' he remarks of the girl whose heart he is about to break. Thus, the world and his people are constantly transformed with his own reflective glow. But Bayayoko is not a cloud-treading deity; his strength lies in a realistic location among the flesh and blood of an embattled humanity. The touches of traditional mores and

relationships are subtle but telling; they are never permitted to harbour a suspicion of the exotic but emerge
naturally from the actualities that surround him. Thus,
at the crucial rally in Dakar, just before he mounts the
platform, an old woman comes up to him and asks if he
still has a mother. Bakayoko says he has none. 'From
today on, then' she says simply, 'I will be your mother
...If you stay in Dakar, my son, come to live with me.
There will always be a place for you.'

We are made conscious of a new society in the process
of coming to birth. Sembene's ideology is implicit, he
does not allow its rhetorical intrusion, but makes it
organic to the process of birth. The strategy of struggle
determines the one ideological resolution, translate it
how one will. An egalitarian discipline has been enforced
upon the community by the goals and the ordeals of the
strike, by the knowledge of colonial indignity with its
imposition of an inferior status on the indigene, its
wage-discrimination and inadequate social facilities. In
spite of the talk of books, the widening of foreign knowledge and the usual paraphernalia which accompany the
process of external indoctrination, the emphasis of social
regeneration is carefully laid on the intrinsic ethical
properties of existing society, their adaptation and universal relations. Key events are brought into being by this
adaptive process, making both of revolution and the
emerging social structures a growth process which can
be described as truly indigenous. So the trial of Diara the
strike-breaker develops, both in its origination and its
resolution, into a process of education for the entire
community.

The agonising of Tiemoko, secretary of the strike
committee in Bamako is symbolic of the whole process.
His meticulous preparation, coupled with his doubts
over the trial of the elderly Diara is pathetic and even
comic, but it is much like the anguish of birth. The
earlier measures against strike-breakers have proved

inadequate; commando squads for administering beat-
ings to the recalcitrant seem temporary and artificial;
Tiemoko instinctively gropes towards the seminal. He
finds it in the missing practices of his people, guided
towards this appreciation by an adherence to traditional
codes of conduct in which he finds no contradiction to
Bakayoko's selective lessons from external wisdoms. 'It
is not necessary to be right to argue,' he intones like a
litany, 'but to win it is necessary both to be right and never
to falter.' The phrase is from his foreign catalogue, but
simultaneously he refused to depart from norms which
represent for him a traditional foundation of communal
cohesion:

> Look, Sadio, your father is my father's brother; you
> are my cousin. Your honour is also mine; your
> family's shame is my family's, and the same of our
> whole country, the dishonour of all our families
> together. That is why we cannot beat your father.
> *(God's Bits of Wood,* p. 120)

This refusal, however, is later revealed not to be a
nepotist compromise; it derives from the appropriateness of the nature of punishment to the notion of the
human being as inseparable from his social context, not
as a cipher in a revolutionary formula. Diara's son indeed
considers the alternative punishment far more severe
than the beating. 'I'd rather die' he declares. For his part
Tiemoko, who has set the entire process in motion and
brings it to a conclusion, declares to Bakayoko's father
(and we believe him):

> If it was my own father, I would do it Fa Keita; I
> swear it on the tomb of my ancestors! And if it were
> you, Ibrahim Bakayoko would do the same thing.
> (p. 123)

When at last he has convinced his colleagues on the
committee of the appropriateness of this methods, he

bursts aloud into an ancient Bambara hymn to the founder of the empire of Mali, the Soundiata. We are being inducted into the founding of an ideological state, drawing upon the humane structures and ethics of the past. The mutual complementarity is constant; Sembene, drawing educative attention to the positive values of a 'way of thinking' among the *toubabs* (the white foreigners) founds his new society on the positive in traditional consciousness. The famous tribunal which is convened from Tiemoko's recollection of similar practices from 'a book written in the white man's language' leaves the pronouncement of a verdict to traditional wisdom, impressively and effectively. Fa Keita, who proposes that verdict, is only incidentally a deeply religious man, a Moslem, and the antithesis of the fat-living collaborator El Hadki Mabigue. The proceedings are kept secular. Fa Keita's utterance at that trial borrows nothing from religious wisdom but from a shrewd human psychology and a belief in the vanishing values of a traditional 'framework, an order that was our own', the existence of which was 'of great importance in our lives.' He strikes the right chord and the community silently adopts his verdict.

As with most writing that concerns itself with the process of an organic revolution, the colonial agents, though they form an important component of the conflict, are paid only grudging attention. Their appearance is reduced in scale to enlarge the positive emergence of the indigenous. Though their presence and actions lay the ground for the conflict, they are reduced to the proportional relations of catalysts; their fate is of no interest to the author except in so far as it may by contrast illuminate the virtues of the new vision of society. Sembene is a contrast here to Ayi Kwei Armah whose weeding operation for the foundations of the new city gives venomous prominence to the existence of the alien obstacle. Not even the sadism of the racial mongrel

Bernadini survives the overwhelming reality of Sembene's community of the Savanah. The stoicism of his victims is the lasting image, as was their weakness and internal treachery in the confrontation with colonial repression. Sembene's sole concession to the justice of retribution appears to be couched – again in contrast to Armah – in the objective illustration provided by the denouement of the march on the 'Vatican', the European quarters, namely, that the colonial oppressor carries with him the seeds of his own destruction. In succeeding so well in making the white presence irrelevant to the deeper processes of a people's history and the reformulation of their interrupted identity, Sembene appears to bear out the words of the Legend of Gouba, the song with which, significantly, he ends the novel:

> From one sun to another
> The combat lasted,
> And fighting together, blood-covered
> They transfixed their enemies
> But happy is the man who does battle without hatred. (p. 333)

We will use Camara Laye to sum up this process of artistic retrieval, though a number of African critics have succeeded in making his work controversial. To recapitulate briefly, the secular imagination re-creates existing mythology (or demonology according to Stoddard). Since even the most esoteric world of symbols, ethics, and values must originate somewhere, the authentic images of African reality give such writers a decisive imaginative liberation. They are familiar and closest to hand; they are not governed by rigid orthodoxies such as obtain in Islamic- and Christian-orientated matrices of symbols; a natural syncretism and the continuing process of this activity is the reality of African metaphysical systems; the protean nature of the symbols of African metaphysics, whether expressed in the idiom of deities, nature events, matter or artifacts, are an obvious boon to the full flow of the imagination. These are sufficient reasons why the African writer has begun to genuflect less and less towards the Islamic or Christian literary altars in spite of their undeniable attractions. The grounding of the writer's societal explorations and their expositions, his historic bearings and visionary exploration cannot for long ignore this private harvest, indeed, the process has already begun. Camara Laye's infusion of the mystic properties of the very instruments of craft, the manifested relationship between flesh, word, activity and the objective world creates a total cosmogonic harmony throughout his elegiac work *The Dark Child* (Collins, 1955). It is a deft exposition of the African world-view and differs radically from the other world-views to which we have already referred. If it were at all possible we would use this expression, 'world-view' in preference to 'religion' wherever the aesthetic revelations of this literature come under consideration, for the former expression is more evocative of fundamental cosmogonic acceptances, especially for the African reality. In contrast to what would be called strictly religious processes in other societies, the harmonisation of human functions, external phenomena and supernatural suppositions within individual consciousness emerges as a normal self-adjusting process in the African temper of mind. Where, for instance, the mediation of ritual is required, it is performed as a human (communal) activity, not as a space-directed act of worship. This is what leads to a preference for a 'world-view', a cosmic totalism, rather than 'religion'. And the literature that is based on this conception differs from others by betraying an exaltation of constantly revolving relationships between man and his environment above a rigid pattern of existence mandated by exteriorised deities.

Less obviously than in his earlier work *The Dark Child,*

The Radiance of the King marks the summative exposition of this view.[4] Casting an outsider, Clarence, in the
central role, Camara Laye proceeds to draw out a quintessence of values from a far larger and certainly more
varied world-view of traditional Africa than was possible
in his semi-autobiographical novel. The process carries
an implicit revaluation, a revolutionary undertaking in
the context of existing literature on Africa at its time. The
device itself is a reversal of the expected; the explorer
into the African unknown is an anti-hero, a counter-
Shrobenius figure who is not permitted to interpret the
continent to its inhabitants. The territory remains unlocated, anthropological specificities are ignored; Camara
Laye's private mythology fills up the terrain, utilising
credible norms of social relationships. The central event
is really a process of education: Clarence's Western form
of rationality cannot be applied to the systems he encounters; his values are useless, his skills irrelevant. Yet
the system works for the members of the community, it
demonstrably harmonises, it offers fulfilment for the
individual within the society and binds man and his
environment into a complementary existence. Clarence
finds that his self-evaluation bears no correspondence to
the needs and judgement of this strange environment.
His self-esteem is gradually eroded, his price falls
rapidly, until at last he is prepared to accept any task
however menial – 'even a drummer-boy'. His education
is, however, still incomplete. Drumming, he learns, is a
highly complex art, involving careful selection, training
and hierarchies, including its functional integration into
the comprehensive understanding of society. Above all,
it delves into the essence of things from which alone the
apparent, the concrete can take meaning. And how can
he, a white (alien) sensibility, hope ever to elicit from the
drum that inner world of meaning. Unlocalised though

[4] Camara Laye, *The Radiance of the King*, translated by James
Kirkup, Collins, London, 1956.

the terrain of action is, Camara Laye employs such expositional devices of art and functionality to flesh out his mysterious African world. The ceremonials of kingship serve this end, among others. So is the creative credo of Diallo the blacksmith, a little self-consciously perhaps, but nevertheless part of the attempt to evoke the 'essential' dimension of creative manifestations such as for example, underlies the figuration of a deity in African sculpture.

Purged finally of most of his cultural accretions, Clarence discovers that what he has been led to believe was a period of impatient but comfortable expectation of the king was indeed the period of his productivity. Unknown to him, he has already fulfilled his destiny in his new society, that of a stud in the harem of the naba, to whom a wily beggar had sold him as a slave. A tempting interpretation of this episode is that Clarence has merely fulfilled the historic destiny of the white coloniser, the spreading of blotches of miscegenated culture on the continent. Or perhaps Camara Laye has set out to give a twist to the sermons of cultural symbiosis such as Senghor's, so that the leaven is now white (and still metallic?) and the dough black.

The realities of this African world are by no means deodorised, though the language of mundane trivia often acquires hints of mystical import. Camara Laye's central objective is the re-establishment of a cohesive cultural reality, with its implicit validation and imperviousness to explication through external world-views. The logic that holds discourse together is an admixture of Zen and the gnomic utterances of African divination – Ifa perhaps? Penetration of Laye's African world is possible only from a passive immersion in its reality; each seemingly disparate manifestation of that reality is indispensable to its fullness of separation from the occidental world, and from the traditional one-dimensional conception of African reality, a largely anthropological creation. This latter attribute of Laye's reconstruction is as important, clearly, to the author as its confrontation with a Western sense of reality. The point has been missed by several of Camara Laye's critics: or perhaps not. The implicit challenge even to the indigene of the African world is perhaps unacceptable, namely that he delve deeper into the essence of what he so readily takes for granted. It threatens his own imaginative security, his confident sense of identification and belonging. William Conton's world in *The African* is, for such critics, a truer world, less demanding, verifiable from statistics in tourist brochures.

Some of the strictures against Laye's work are of course only too true. Parts of the novel are too derivative, especially from Kafka. A critic at a conference table once let out an anguished cry which I recognised as coming from the heart: 'But how can an African write like Kafka?' The answer is, why not? But that does not make it necessary to be so derivative that one can, as in *The Radiance of the King,* actually point to character transpositions. But that critic's prescription for the anti-Kafkaesque was, like that of Camara Laye's most persistent critics in *Presence Africaine,* the presentation of African society where every piece of thatch is clearly delineated and every royal praise-song available in UNESCO recordings. *The Radiance of the King* transcends the merely apparent, the pecks at anthropology, to construct a quasi-mythological existence with the essence of reality. In presenting a lost or hidden model it poses a paradigm of the deeper African reality, a mysterious and complex paradigm in opposition to the simplistic and the naturalistic, the immediately accessible. In one of his rare replies to his critics (*Africa Report,* 17 May 1972) Camara Laye asserts that he has concerned himself with eliciting certain values from traditional African society. By highlighting these in affirmation of black civilisation, he was, he felt, initiating a process of revaluation which was itself revolutionary in the anti-colonial situation. This was said in reference to *L'Enfant Noir*. 'What concerns me most is the timeless quality of the specific values of our culture'. The elicitation of that 'timeless quality' is the methodology of the latter work. Despite the mystical effusion at the end, the aesthetics of the novel are secular, based on the harmonies of social relationships and human functions. *The Radiance of the King* remains our earliest imaginative effort towards a modern literary aesthetic that is unquestionably African, and secular.

The question must now be confronted: How comes it then that despite the extolled self-apprehending virtues of these and other works, it is possible to entertain a hostile attitude towards the programmatic summation in the secular vision of Negritude? There is none of these works whose ideals may not be interpreted as the realisation of the principles of race-retrieval which are embodied in the concept of Negritude, yet Negritude continues to arouse more than a mere semantic impatience among the later generation of African writers and intellectuals, in addition to – let this be remembered – serious qualifications of, or tactical withdrawal from the full conception of Negritude by a number of writers who assisted at its origin.

The vision of Negritude should never be underestimated or belittled. What went wrong with it is contained in what I earlier expressed as the contrivance of a creative ideology and its falsified basis of identification with the social vision. This vision in itself was that of restitution and re-engineering of a racial psyche, the establishment of a distinct human entity and the glorification of its long-suppressed attributes. (On an even longer-term basis, as universal alliance with the world's dispossessed.) In attempting to achieve this laudable goal however, Negritude proceeded along the route of over-simplification. Its re-entrenchment of black values was not preceded by any profound effort to enter into this African system of values. It extolled the apparent. Its reference points took far too much colouring from European ideas even while its Messiahs pronounced themselves fanatically African. In attempting to refute the evaluation to which black reality had been subjected, Negritude adopted the Manichean tradition of European thought and inflicted it on a culture which is most radically anti-Manichean. It not only accepted the dialectical structure of European ideological confrontations but borrowed from the very components of its racist syllogism.

By way of elaboration, let us extend Sartre's grading of Negritude as 'the minor term of a dialectical progression'. The 'theoretical and practical assertion of the supremacy of the white man is its thesis; the position of negritude as an antithetical value is the bottom of negativity'.[5] This was the position in which Negritude found itself; we will now pose a pair of syllogisms from the racist philosophy that provoked it into being:

(a) Analytical thought is a mark of high human development.
The European employs analytical thought.
Therefore the European is highly developed.

(b) Analytical thought is a mark of high human development.
The African is incapable of analytical thought.
Therefore the African is not highly developed.

(For 'analytical thought' substitute scientific inventiveness etc.)

[5] This and other quotations from Sartre are from his essay 'Orphée Noir', preface to Leopold Senghor (ed.), *Anthologie de la Nouvelle Poésie Négre et Malagache d'Expression Francaise*, Presses Universitaires de France, 1948.

The dialectic progression in history of these two syllogisms need not be dwelt upon: the European is highly developed, the African is not, therefore etc. Slavery and colonialism took their basic justification from such palpably false premises. But the temper of the times (both the liberal conscience of Europe and the new assertiveness of the victims of Eurocentric dialectics) required a re-phrasing of premises and conclusions – preferably of course, even for liberal Europe, the conclusions only. Negritude strangely lent approval to this partial methodology, accepting in full the premises of both syllogisms and the conclusion of *(a)*, justifying Sartre's commentary that the theoretical and practical assertion of the supremacy of the white man was the tacitly adopted thesis, and failing utterly to demolish it. The conclusion of *(a)* was never challenged, though attempts were made to give new definitions to what constitutes high development. The method there was to reconstruct *(b)* altogether, while leaving *(a)* intact. This was the initial error. Negritude did not bother to free the black races from the burden of its acceptance. Even the second premise of *(a)*, 'The European employs analytical thought', is falsely posed, for it already implies a racial separatism which provides the main argument. Is the entire exercise not rendered futile if we substituted for this, 'Man is capable of analytical thought'? The Negritudinists did not; they accepted the battleground of Eurocentric prejudices and racial chauvinism, and moved to replace syllogism *(b)* with an amended version:

(c) Intuitive understanding is *also* a mark of human development.
The African employs intuitive understanding.
Therefore the African is highly developed.

(For 'intuitive understanding' substitute the dance, rhythm etc.)

The dialectic progression which moved, logically enough, from this amendment, positing the attractive universality of Negritude, was based on *(a)* and *(c)*, resulting in a symbiotic human culture – the black leaven in the white metallic loaf. How could the mistake ever have been made that the new propositions in *(c)* wiped away the inherent insult of *(b)*, which was merely a development of the racist assumptions of *(a)?* They said, oh yes, the Gobineaus of the world are right; Africans neither think nor construct, but it doesn't matter because – voilà! – they intuit! And so they moved to construct a romantic edifice, confident that its rhythmic echoes would drown the repugnant conclusion of proposition *(b)*, which of course simply refused to go away. How could it, when its premises were constantly reinforced by affirmations such as this:

> Emotive sensitivity. Emotion is completely Negro as reason is Greek. Water rippled by every breeze? Unsheltered soul blown by every wind, whose fruit often drops before it is ripe? Yes, in one way, *The Negro is richer in gifts than in works!*[6]

This is not, judging by the literature and the tracts which emerged from Negritude, an unfair extract. Negritude trapped itself in what was primarily a defensive role, even though its accents were strident, its syntax hyperbolic and its strategy aggressive. It accepted one of the most commonplace blasphemies of racism, that the black man has nothing between his ears, and proceeded to subvert the power of poetry to glorify this fabricated justification of European cultural domination. Suddenly, we were exhorted to give a cheer for those who never invented anything, a cheer for those who never explored the oceans. The truth, however, is that there isn't any such creature. An even more distressing deduction which escaped the euphoricists of such negativism is that they,

[6] Italics and exclamation mark mine, the rest Senghor's.

poets, had turned themselves into laudators of creative truncation. They suggest something which is indeed alien to the African world-view: that there are watertight categories of the creative spirit, that creativity is not one smooth-flowing source of human regeneration. The very idea of separating the manifestations of the human genius is foreign to the African world-view. Self-subjugation to the actual artifacts which man has himself created is of course something else, and is equally alien to the African creative spirit, but the Negritudinists were not referring to that. Their propaganda for creative separatism went much deeper. And one of its unfortunate by-products was a mounting narcissism which involved contemplation of the contrived self in the supposed tragic grandeur of the cultural dilemma. Thus, admittedly at the bottom regions of such poetry, we encountered:

> Here we stand
> infants overblown
> poised between two civilisations
> finding the balance irksome
> itching for something to happen
> to tip us one way or the other
> groping in the dark for a helping hand
> and finding none.
> I'm tired, O my God, I'm tired,
> I'm tired of hanging in the middle way –
> but where can I go?[7]

Some critics, through taking this kind of versification more seriously than could be warranted by language or composition, try to see in it a certain phase of development to which Negritude gave the decisive answer. Adrian Roscoe makes this suggestion in his *Mother is Gold*.[8] I disagree. This kind of poetry was of course a

[7] Mabel Segun in Frances Ademola (ed.), *Reflections*, African Universities Press, Lagos, 1962, p. 65.

[8] Roscoe, *Mother is Gold*, Cambridge University Press, 1971.

product of Negritude, but not of its practitioners. The dilemma is self-conscious. The question at the tail-end of the poem sounds rhetorical, as if the writer has no real interest in the answer. It was part of a totally artificial angst fabricated by a handful of writers *after* Negritude revealed to them the very seductive notion that they had to commence a search for their Africanness. Until then, they were never even aware that it was missing. The opportunity to create a lot of mileage out of this potentially tragic loss was too great to miss; unfortunately, as in the above example, it was not always matched by the poetic talent.

This was one of the unfortunate by-products of Negritude, the abysmal angst of low achievement. By contrast there were exquisite nuggets of lyric celebration in these excavations of the vanishing racial psyche, such as the following familiar lines of Birago Diop. They are some of the best to have come from the Negritudinist movement because the conviction they carry is self-evident. The poem is not a manifesto in verse-form, nor does it pretend to be the summation of the cosmogonic view which gave rise to it. It may occasionally sound proselytising, as indeed most of the poetry of this movement does, but it is the quiet enthusiasm of the initiate, the sharing instinct of the votive who has experienced immersion in a particular dimension of reality and calls out from within his spiritual repletion. Because of its unusual lyrical possession by an integral reality of the African world, I shall quote it in full.

Breath

Listen more to things
Than to words that are said.
The water's voice sings
And the flame cries
And the wind that brings
The woods to sighs
Is the breathing of the dead.

Those who are dead have never gone away.
They are in the shadows darkening around,
They are in the shadows fading into day,
The dead are not under the ground.
They are in the trees that quiver,
They are in the woods that weep,
They are in the waters of the rivers,
They are in the waters that sleep.
They are in the crowds, they are in the homestead.
The dead are never dead.

Listen more to things
Than to words that are said.
The water's voice sings
And the flame cries
And the wind that brings
The woods to sighs
Is the breathing of the dead.
Who have not gone away
Who are not under the ground
Who are never dead.

Those who are dead have never gone away.
They are at the breast of the wife.
They are in the child's cry of dismay
And the firebrand bursting into life.
The dead are not under the ground.
They are in the fire that burns low
They are in the grass with tears to shed,
In the rock where whining winds blow
They are in the forest, they are in the homestead.
The dead are never dead.

Listen more to things
Than to words that are said.
The water's voice sings
And the flame cries
And the wind that brings

The woods to sighs
Is the breathing of the dead.

And repeats each day
The Covenant where it is said
That our fate is bound to the law,
And the fated of the dead who are not dead
To the spirits of breath who are stronger than they.
We are bound to Life by this harsh law
And by this Covenant we are bound
To the deeds of the breathings that die
Along the bed and the banks of the river,
To the deeds of the breaths that quiver
In the rock that whines and the grasses that cry
To the deeds of the breathings that lie
In the shadow that lightens and grows deep
In the tree that shudders, in the woods that weep,
In the waters that flow and the waters that sleep,
To the spirits of breath which are stronger than they
That have taken the breath of the deathless dead
Of the dead who have never gone away
Of the dead who are not now under the ground.

Listen more to things
Than to words that are said.
The water's voice sings
And the flame cries
And the wind that brings
The woods to sighs
Is the breathing of the dead.[9]

Now such a poem conveys an important, even fundamental aspect of the world-view of traditional Africa and
remains within this mandate. Diop does not suggest here
that the African could not manufacture tools to help him
dig a grave to inter the body of this undead dead, nor

[9] *French African Verse*, translated by John Reed and Clive Wake,
Heinemann, 1964, p. 25. The poem *Souffles* ('Breath') appears in
Birago Diop's *Leurres et Lueurs*, published by *Présence Africaine*, Paris
(1960).

that every medical effort is not made to keep the body alive until it is too late. Nor that the sickness and the treatment are determined by intuition rather than through long-evolved systems of medical research and practice, herbal, surgical and psychiatric. Unfortunately the bulk of Negritudinist poets were not content to confine their re-definition of society in this way.

It should not surprise us that the most dogmatic statements about the potential vision of Negritude were made by European intellectuals. And such statements are an ideological stab in the back. There was a kind of poetic justice in this. Negritude, having laid its cornerstone on a European intellectual tradition, however bravely it tried to reverse its concepts (leaving its tenets untouched), was a foundling deserving to be drawn into, nay, even considered a case for benign adoption by European ideological interests. That it was something which should exist in its own right, which deserved to be considered a product and a vindication of a separate earth and civilisation did not occur to Jean-Paul Sartre who, proposing the toast of Negritude proceeded literally to drink it under the table. It was not difficult. Negritude was already intoxicated by its own presumptions.

> Negritude is the low ebb in a dialectical progression. The theoretical and practical assertion of white supremacy is the thesis; negritude's role as an antithetical value is the negative stage. But this negative stage will not satisfy the Negroes who are using it, and they are well aware of this. They know that they are aiming for human synthesis or fulfilment in a raceless society. Negritude is destined to destroy itself; it is the path and the goal, the means but not the end.

As Fanon cried out in anguish: 'And so, it is not I who make a meaning for myself, but it is the meaning that was already there, pre-existing, waiting for me.'

134

And what is this end which Sartre envisages? The transcendence over racial concepts and alignment with the proletarian struggle. Like all ideologues who ignore the existence or pretend the non-existence of factors which do not fit into the framework of an ideological projection, Sartre ignores the important fact that Negritude was a creation by and for a small élite. The search for a racial identity was conducted by and for a minuscule minority of uprooted individuals, not merely in Paris but in the metropolis of the French colonies. At the same time as this historical phenomenon was taking place, a drive through the real Africa, among the real populace of the African world would have revealed that these millions had never at any time had cause to question the existence of their – Negritude. This is why, even in a country like Senegal where Negritude is the official ideology of the régime, it remains a curiosity for the bulk of the population and an increasingly shopworn and dissociated expression even among the younger intellectuals and litterateurs.

As for the pipe-dream of Sartre that it would pass through stages of development and merge itself within the context of the proletarian fight, one would have thought that it was obvious enough that Negritude was the property of a bourgeois–intellectual élite, and that there was therefore far greater likelihood that it would become little more than a diversionary weapon in the eventual emergence of a national revolutionary struggle wherever the flag-bearers of Negritude represent the power-holding elite. Sartre was not being naive, however. He had merely, as would any confident ideologue, classified this colonial movement as springing from the intellectual conditioning of the mother culture; he rightly assumed that any movement founded on an antithesis which responded to the Cartesian 'I think, therefore I am' with 'I feel, therefore I am' must be subject to a dialectical determinism which made all those who 'are' obedient to laws formulated on the European historical experience. How was he to know, if the proponents of the universal vision of Negritude themselves did not, that the African world did not and need not share the history of civilisations trapped in political Manicheisms? The principle of definition in the African world system is far more circumspect, and constantly avoids the substitution of the temporal or partial function or quality for the essence of an active or inert sociopolitical totality. The fundamental error was one of procedure: Negritude stayed within a pre-set system of Eurocentric intellectual analysis both of man and society and tried to re-define the African and his society in those externalised terms. In the end, even the poetry of celebration for this supposed self-retrieval became indistinguishable from the mainstream of French poetry. The autumn of the flowers of evil had, through a shared tradition of excessive self-regarding, become confused with the spring of African rebirth. Fanon's warning went unheeded:

> To us, the man who adores the Negro is as 'sick' as the man who abominates him.[10]

But this problem does not apply to the Negritudinists alone. African intellectualism in general, and therefore African attitudes to race and culture, have failed to come to grips with the very foundations of Eurocentric epistemology. Let us take this simple but basic example of the syllogistic method of enquiry, one which is applied as readily to mathematical or scientific propositions as to supposed verities ranging from the origin of the universe to the fluctuating prices of oil on the market. The basis of this European intellectual tradition necessarily admits the unprovable or the outright falsity, a fact demonstrated in considerable measure by Europe's analysis and

[10] Franz Fanon, *Black Skin White Masks*, translated by C. L. Markmann, Paladin, London, 1970, p. 8.

conclusions about other cultures and civilisations. This process of intellection requires the propagandist knack of turning the unprovable into an authoritative concept, indoctrinating society into the acceptance of a single, simple criterion as governing any number of human acts and habits, evaluations and even habits of understanding.[11] (Freudianism is one of the most notorious modern examples.) The criterion proliferates, creates its own special language and its micro-world of hierarchic sub-concepts in an internally cohering pattern. The European intellectual temperament appears to be historically conducive to the infiltration of such mono-criteria. It is the responsibility of today's African intellectual not only to question these criteria, but to avoid the conditioning of the social being by the mono-criterion methodology of Europe.

Sartre, for instance, anxious to prove that the idea of race can mingle with that of class, writes:

> the first [race] is concrete and particular, the second is universal and abstract; the one stems from what Jaspers calls understanding and the other from intellection; the first is the result of a psychological syncretism and the second is a methodical construction based on experience.

From this he concludes that Negritude is destined to prepare the 'synthesis or realization of the human in a society without races'. Now let us, from an Afrocentric bias of concepts, examine the contrasting relations posed above. Does the racial self-conception of the African really exclude the process of intellection? More critically, is the reality of African social structure – from which alone 'class' can obtain concrete definition – not a thorough fusion of individual functional relations with

[11] Notes made some years ago, parts of which are lost, suggest that this sentence was actually copied in confirmation of my observations, from a book I was reading at the time, but do not indicate which book.

society, one that cannot be distinguished from a 'psychological syncretism' of self and community, from a mode of self-conceiving that is identical with that of racial belonging? The contrary is not only unprovable but *inconceivable* in the traditional African view of man, and the question then remains: whether this conceptual totalism cannot be rescued from European compartmentalist intellect or must be subsumed by the more assertive culture in the 'realization of the human in a society without races'. The answer, for the Negritudinist, latterly became yes to the second option, predictably. For Negritude, having yielded to the seduction of synthetic European intellectualism, accepted the consequences that befall the junior relation in all dialectic progressions. Possessed, they tried to constrict the protean universalism of the African experience into the obverse monothetical appendage (Sartre calls it anti-thesis, naturally) of a particularised, unprovable and even irrelevant European criterion.

Let us respond, very simply, as I imagine our mythical brother innocent would respond in his virginal village, pursuing his innocent sports, suddenly confronted by the figure of Descartes in his pith-helmet, engaged in the mission of piercing the jungle of the black pre-logical mentality with his intellectual canoe. As our Cartesian ghost introduces himself by scribbling on our black brother's – naturally – *tabula rasa* the famous proposition, 'I think, therefore I am', we should not respond, as the Negritudinists did, with 'I feel, therefore I am', for that is to accept the arrogance of a philosophical certitude that has no foundation in the provable, one which reduces the cosmic logic of being to a functional particularism of being. I cannot imagine that our 'authentic black innocent' would ever have permitted himself to be manipulated into the false position of countering one pernicious Manicheism with another. He would sooner, I suspect, reduce our white explorer to syntactical proportions by responding: 'You think, therefore you are a thinker. You are one-who-thinks, white-creature-in-pith-helmet-in-African-jungle-who-thinks and, finally, white-man-who-has-problems-believing-in-his-own-existence.' And I cannot believe that he would arrive at that observation solely by intuition.

Appendix: The fourth stage

(Through the Mysteries of Ogun[1] to the origin of Yoruba tragedy)

The persistent search for the meaning of tragedy, for a re-definition in terms of cultural or private experience is, at the least, man's recognition of certain areas of depth-experience which are not satisfactorily explained by general aesthetic theories; and, of all the subjective unease that is aroused by man's creative insights, that wrench within the human psyche which we vaguely define as 'tragedy' is the most insistent voice that bids us return to our own sources. There, illusively, hovers the key to the human paradox, to man's experience of being and non-being, his dubiousness as essence and matter, intimations of transience and eternity, and the harrowing drives between uniqueness and Oneness.

Our course to the heart of the Yoruba Mysteries leads by its own ironic truths through the light of Nietzsche[2] and the Phrygian deity; but there are the inevitable, key departures. 'Blessed Greeks!' sings our mad votary in his recessional rapture, 'how great must be your Dionysos, if the Delic god thinks such enchantments necessary to cure you of your Dithyrambic madness.' Such is Apollo's resemblance to the serene art of Obatala[3] the pure unsullied one, to the 'essence' idiom of his rituals, that

[1] Ogun: God of creativity, guardian of the road, god of metallic lore and artistry. Explorer, hunter, god of war, Custodian of the sacred oath.

[2] Nietzsche, *The Birth of Tragedy.*

[3] Obatala: God of creation (by syncretist tradition with Orisa-nla), essence of the serene arts. Obatala moulds the forms but the breath of life is administered by Edumare the Supreme deity. The art of Obatala is thus essentially plastic and formal.

it is tempting to place him at the end of a creative axis with Ogun, in a parallel evolutionary relationship to Nietzsche's Dionysos–Apollo brotherhood. But Obatala the sculptural god is not the artist of Apollonian illusion but of inner essence. The idealist bronze and terra-cotta of Ife which may tempt the comparison implicit in 'Apollonian' died at some now forgotten period, evidence only of the universal surface culture of courts and never again resurrected. It is alien to the Obatala spirit of Yoruba 'essential' art. Obatala finds expression, not in Nietzsche's Apollonian 'mirror of enchantment' but as a statement of world resolution. The mutual tempering of illusion and will, necessary to an understanding of the Hellenic spirit, may mislead us, when we are faced with Yoruba art, for much of it has a similarity in its aesthetic serenity to the plastic arts of the Hellenic. Yoruba traditional art is not ideational however, but 'essential'. It is not the idea (in religious arts) that is transmitted into wood or interpreted in music or movement, but a quintessence of inner being, a symbolic interaction of the many aspects of revelations (within a universal context) with their moral apprehension.

Ogun, for his part, is best understood in Hellenic values as a totality of the Dionysian, Apollonian and Promethean virtues. Nor is that all. Transcending, even today, the distorted myths of his terrorist reputation, traditional poetry records him as 'protector of orphans', 'roof over the homeless', 'terrible guardian of the sacred oath'; Ogun stands for a transcendental, humane but rigidly restorative justice. (Unlike Sango, who is primarily retributive.) The first artist and technician of the forge, he evokes like Nietzsche's Apollonian spirit, a 'massive impact of image, concept, ethical doctrine and sympathy'. Obatala is the placid essence of creation; Ogun the creative urge and instinct, the essence of creativity.

Rich-laden is his home, yet decked in palm fronds
He ventures forth, refuge of the down-trodden,
To rescue slaves he unleashed the judgment of war
Because of the blind, plunged into forests
Of curative herbs, Bountiful One
Who stands bulwark to offsprings of the dead of
heaven
Salutations, O lone being, who swims in rivers of
blood.

Such virtues place Ogun apart from the distorted
dances to which Nietzsche's Dionysiac frenzy led him in
his search for a selective 'Aryan' soul, yet do not detract
from Ogun's revolutionary grandeur. Ironically, it is the
depth-illumination of Nietzsche's intuition into basic
universal impulses which negates his race exclusivist
conclusions on the nature of art and tragedy. In our
journey to the heart of Yoruba tragic art which indeed
belongs in the Mysteries of Ogun and the choric ecstasy
of revellers, we do not find that the Yoruba, as the Greek
did, 'built for his chorus the scaffolding of a fictive
chthonic realm and placed thereon fictive nature spirits
...' on which foundation, claims Nietzsche, Greek
tragedy developed: in short, the principle of illusion.

Yoruba tragedy plunges straight into the 'chthonic
realm', the seething cauldron of the dark world will and
psyche, the transitional yet inchoate matrix of death and
becoming. Into this universal womb once plunged and
emerged Ogun, the first actor, disintegrating within the
abyss. His spiritual re-assemblage does not require a
'copying of actuality' in the ritual re-enactment of his
devotees, any more than Obatala does in plastic representation, in the art of Obatala. The actors in Ogun
Mysteries are the communicant chorus, containing
within their collective being the essence of that transitional abyss. But only as essence, held, contained and
mystically expressed. Within the mystic summons of the

chasm the protagonist actor (and every god-suffused choric individual) resists, like Ogun before him, the final step towards complete annihilation. From this alone steps forward the eternal actor of the tragic rites, first as the unresisting mouthpiece of the god, uttering visions symbolic of the transitional gulf, interpreting the dread power within whose essence he is immersed as agent of the choric will. Only later, in the evenness of release from the tragic climax, does the serene self-awareness of Obatala reassert its creative control. He, the actor, emerges still as the mediant voice of the god, but stands now as it were beside himself, observant, understanding, creating. At this stage is known to him the sublime *aesthetic* joy, not within Nietzsche's heart of original oneness but in the distanced celebration of the cosmic struggle. This resolved aesthetic serenity is the link between Ogun's tragic art and Obatala's plastic beauty. The unblemished god, Obatala, is the serene womb of chthonic reflections (or memory), a passive strength awaiting and celebrating each act of vicarious restoration of his primordial being. (We shall come later to the story of that first severance.) His beauty is enigmatic, expressive only of the resolution of plastic healing through the wisdom of acceptance. Obatala's patient suffering is the well-known aesthetics of the saint.

For the Yoruba, the gods are the final measure of eternity, as humans are of earthly transience. To think, because of this, that the Yoruba mind reaches intuitively towards absorption in godlike essence is to misunderstand the principle of religious rites, and to misread, as many have done, the significance of religious possession. Past, present and future being so pertinently conceived and woven into the Yoruba world view, the element of eternity which is the gods' prerogative does not have the same quality of remoteness or exclusiveness which it has in Christian or Buddhist culture. The belief of the Yoruba in the contemporaneous existence within his daily experience of these aspects of time has long been recognised but again misinterpreted. It is no abstraction. The Yoruba is not, like European man, concerned with the purely conceptual aspects of time; they are too concretely realised in his own life, religion, sensitivity, to be mere tags for explaining the metaphysical order of his world. If we may put the same thing in fleshed-out cognitions, life, present life, contains within it manifestations of the ancestral, the living and the unborn. All are vitally within the intimations and affectiveness of life, beyond mere abstract conceptualisation.

And yet the Yoruba does not for that reason fail to distinguish between himself and the deities, between himself and the ancestors, between the unborn and his reality, or discard his awareness of the essential gulf that lies between one area of existence and another. This gulf is what must be constantly diminished by the sacrifices, the rituals, the ceremonies of appeasement to those cosmic powers which lie guardian to the gulf. Spiritually, the primordial disquiet of the Yoruba psyche may be expressed as the existence in collective memory of a primal severance in transitional ether,[4] whose first effective defiance is symbolised in the myth of the gods' descent to earth and the battle with immense chaotic growth which had sealed off reunion with man. For they were coming down, not simply to be acknowledged but to be re-united with human essence, to reassume that portion of re-creative transient awareness which the first deity Orisa-nla possessed and expressed through his continuous activation of man images – brief reflections of divine facets – just as man is grieved by a consciousness of the loss of the eternal essence of his being and must

[4] I would render this more cogently today in terms of race origination, uprooting, wandering and settling. This group experience is less remote, and parallels the mythology of primordial chaos, as well as the rites of transition (birth, death etc.). See reference to Sango's drama in chapter 2.

indulge in symbolic transactions to recover his totality of being.

Tragedy, in Yoruba traditional drama, is the anguish of this severance, the fragmentation of essence from self. Its music is the stricken cry of man's blind soul as he flounders in the void and crashes through a deep abyss of a-spirituality and cosmic rejection. Tragic music is an echo from that void; the celebrant speaks, sings and dances in authentic archetypal images from within the abyss. All understand and respond, for it is the language of the world.

It is necessary to emphasise that the gods were coming down to be reunited with man, for this tragedy could not be, the anguish of severance would not attain such tragic proportions, if the gods' position on earth (i.e. in man's conception) was to be one of divine remoteness. This is again testified to by the form of worship, which is marked by camaraderie and irreverence just as departure to ancestorhood is marked by bawdiness in the midst of grief. The anthropomorphic origin of uncountable deities is one more leveller of divine class-consciousness but, finally, it is the innate humanity of the gods themselves, their bond with man through a common animist relation with nature and phenomena. Continuity for the Yoruba operates both through the cyclic concept of time and the animist interfusion of all matter and consciousness.

The first actor – for he led the others – was Ogun, first suffering deity, first creative energy, the first challenger, and conqueror of transition. And his, the first art, was tragic art, for the complementary drama of the syncretic successor to Orisa-nla, Obatala's 'Passion' play, is only the plastic resolution of Ogun's tragic engagement. The Yoruba metaphysics of accommodation and resolution could only come after the passage of the gods through the transitional gulf, after the demonic test of the self-will of Ogun the explorer-god in the creative cauldron of cosmic powers. Only after such testing could the harmonious Yoruba world be born, a harmonious will which accommodates every alien material or abstract phenomenon within its infinitely stressed spirituality. The artifact of Ogun's conquest of separation, the 'fetish', was iron ore, symbol of earth's womb-energies, cleaver and welder of life. Ogun, through his redemptive action became the first symbol of the alliance of disparities when, from earth itself, he extracted elements for the subjugation of chthonic chaos. In tragic consciousness the votary's psyche reaches out beyond the realm of nothingness (or spiritual chaos) which is potentially destructive of human awareness, through areas of terror and blind energies into a ritual empathy with the gods, the eternal presence, who once preceded him in parallel awareness of their own incompletion. Ritual anguish is therefore experienced as that primal transmission of the god's despair – vast, numinous, always incomprehensible. In vain we seek to capture it in words; there is only for the protagonist the certainty of the experience of this abyss – the tragic victim plunges into it in spite of ritualistic earthing and is redeemed only by action. Without acting, and yet in spite of it he is forever lost in the maul of tragic tyranny.

Acting is therefore a contradiction of the tragic spirit, yet it is also its natural complement. To act, the Promethean instinct of rebellion, channels anguish into a creative purpose which releases man from a totally destructive despair, releasing from within him the most energetic, deeply combative inventions which, without usurping the territory of the infernal gulf, bridges it with visionary hopes. Only the battle of the will is thus primally creative; from its spiritual stress springs the soul's despairing cry which proves its own solace, which alone reverberating within the cosmic vaults usurps (at least, and however briefly) the powers of the abyss. At the charged climactic moments of the tragic rites we understand how music came to be the sole art form which can contain tragic reality. The votary is led by no other guide into the pristine heart of tragedy. Music as the embodiment of the tragic spirit has been more than perceptively exhausted in the philosophy of Europe; there is little to add, much to qualify. And the function and nature of music in Yoruba tragedy is peculiarly revealing of the shortcomings of long accepted conclusions of European intuition.

The European concept of music does not fully illuminate the relationship of music to ritual and drama among the Yoruba. We are inhibited even by recognition of a universality of concepts in the European intuitive grasp of the emotions of the will. First, it is 'unmusical' to separate Yoruba musical form from myth and poetry. The nature of Yoruba music is intensively the nature of its language and poetry, highly charged, symbolic, myth-embryonic. We acknowledge quite readily the technical lip-service paid to the correspondence of African music to the tonal patterns (meaning and allusion) of the language, but the aesthetic and emotional significance of this relationship has not been truly absorbed, one which springs from the primal simultaneity of art-forms in a culture of total awareness and phenomenal involvement. Language therefore is not a barrier to the profound universality of music but a cohesive dimension and clarification of that wilfully independent art-form which we label music. Language reverts in religious rites to its pristine existence, eschewing the sterile limits of particularisation. In cult funerals, the circle of initiate mourners, an ageless swaying grove of dark pines, raises a chant around a mortar of fire, and words are taken back to their roots, to their original poetic sources when fusion was total and the movement of words was the very passage of music and the dance of images. Language is still the embryo of thought and music where myth is daily companion, for there language is constantly mythopoeic.

Language in Yoruba tragic music therefore undergoes transformation through myth into a secret (masonic) correspondence with the symbolism of tragedy, a symbolic medium of spiritual emotions within the heart of the choric union. It transcends particularisation (of meaning) to tap the tragic source whence spring the familiar weird disruptive melodies. This masonic union of sign and melody, the true tragic music, unearths cosmic uncertainties which pervade human existence, reveals the magnitude and power of creation, but above all creates a harrowing sense of omni-directional vastness where the creative Intelligence resides and prompts the soul to futile exploration. The senses do not at such moments interpret myth in their particular concretions; we are left only with the emotional and spiritual values, the essential experience of cosmic reality. The forms of music are not correspondences at such moments to the physical world, not at this nor at any other moment. The singer is a mouthpiece of the chthonic forces of the matrix and his somnabulist 'improvisations' – a simultaneity of musical and poetic forms – are not representations of the ancestor, recognitions of the living or unborn, but of the no man's land of transition between and around these temporal definitions of experience. The past is the ancestors', the present belongs to the living, and the future to the unborn. The deities stand in the same situation to the living as do the ancestors and the unborn, obeying the same laws, suffering the same agonies and uncertainties, employing the same masonic intelligence of rituals for the perilous plunge into the fourth area of experience, the immeasurable gulf of transition. Its dialogue is liturgy, its music takes form from man's uncomprehending immersion in this area of existence, buried wholly from rational recognition. The source of the possessed lyricist, chanting hitherto unknown mythopoeic strains whose antiphonal refrain is, however, instantly caught and thrust with all its terror and awesomeness into the night by swaying votaries, this source is residual in the numinous area of transition.

This is the fourth stage, the vortex of archetypes and home of the tragic spirit.

It is necessary to recall again that the past is not a mystery and that although the future (the unborn) is yet unknown, it is not a mystery to the Yoruba but co-existent in present consciousness. Tragic terror exists therefore neither in the evocation of the past nor of the future. The stage of transition is, however, the metaphysical abyss both of god and man, and if we agree that, in the European sense, music is the 'direct copy or the direct expression of the will', it is only because nothing rescues man (ancestral, living or unborn) from loss of self within this abyss but a titanic resolution of the will whose ritual summons, response, and expression is the strange alien sound to which we give the name of music. On the arena of the living, when man is stripped of excrescences, when disasters and conflicts (the material of drama) have crushed and robbed him of self-consciousness and pretensions, he stands in present reality at the spiritual edge of this gulf, he has nothing left in physical existence which successfully impresses upon his spiritual or psychic perception. It is at such moments that transitional memory takes over and intimations rack him of that intense parallel of his progress through the gulf of transition, of the dissolution of his self and his struggle and triumph over subsumation through the agency of will. It is this experience that the modern tragic dramatist recreates through the medium of physical contemporary action, reflecting emotions of the first active battle of the will through the abyss of dissolution.[5] Ogun is the first

[5] Or again the collective memory of dispersion and re-assemblage in racial coming-into-being. All these, and of course the recurring experience of birth and death, are psycho-historic motifs for the tragic experience: the essence of transition.

actor in that battle, and Yoruba tragic drama is the re-enactment of the cosmic conflict.

To recognise why Ogun was elected for his role (and the penalty of horror which he had to pay for his challenge) is to penetrate the symbolism of Ogun both as essence of anguish and as combative will within the cosmic embrace of the transitional gulf. We have said that nothing but the will (for that alone is left untouched) rescues being from annihilation within the abyss. Ogun is embodiment of Will, and the Will is the paradoxical truth of destructiveness and creativeness in acting man. Only one who has himself undergone the experience of disintegration, whose spirit has been tested and whose psychic resources laid under stress by the forces most inimical to individual assertion, only he can understand and be the force of fusion between the two contradictions. The resulting sensibility is also the sensibility of the artist, and he is a profound artist only to the degree to which he comprehends and expresses this principle of destruction and re-creation.

We must not lose sight of the fact that Ogun is the artistic spirit, and not in the sentimental sense in which rhapsodists of negritude would have us conceive the negro as pure artistic intuition. The significant creative truth of Ogun is affirmation of the re-creative intelligence; this is irreconcilable with naive intuition. The symbolic artifact of his victory is metallic ore, at once a technical medium as it is symbolic of deep earth energies, a fusion of elemental energies, a binding force between disparate bodies and properties. Thus Ogun, tragic actor, primordial voice of creative man is also, without a contradiction of essences, the forerunner and ancestor of palaeotechnic man. The principle of creativity when limited to pastoral idyllism, as negritude has attempted to limit it, shuts us off from the deeper, fundamental resolutions of experience and cognition. The tragic actor for the future age (already the present for Europe) is that neo-technic ancestor Sango,[6] god of electricity, whose tragedy stems similarly from the principle of a preliminary self-destruction, represented (as in a later penalty of Ogun) in the blind ignorant destruction of his own flesh and blood. What, for Ogun, was a destructive penalty leading to a secondary drama of 'Passion' was in Sango the very core of his tragedy. The historic process of dilution in tragic challenge is manifested in the relationship of these two myths. Sango is an anthropomorphic deity; his history revolved around petty tyranny; his self-destruction was the violent, central explosion from ego-inflation. Where Ogun's human alienation was the postscript error, an exaction for his basic victory over the transitional guardians of the gulf, Sango's was 'in character', a wild vengeful slaughter upon menials who had dared to defy his authority. But the 'terror and pity' of Sango is undeniable, only it is the 'terror and pity' of human disavowal for that new disciple standing on the edge of the sublimating abyss already subdued by Ogun. We will not find the roots of tragedy in the Mysteries of Sango.

Yoruba myth is a recurrent exercise in the experience of disintegration, and this is significant for the seeming distancing of will among a people whose mores, culture and metaphysics are based on apparent resignation and acceptance but which are, experienced in depth, a statement of man's penetrating insight into the final resolution of things and the constant evidence of harmony. What moral values do we encounter in the drama of Obatala, representative though it also is of the first disintegration experienced by godhead? We are further back in Origin, not now engaged in the transitional battle

[6] Sango: God of lightning and electricity. A tyrant of Oyo, he was forced to commit suicide by factions, through his own over-reaching. His followers thereupon deified him and he assumed the agency of lightning.

of Ogun, but in the fragmentation of Orisa-nla, the primal deity, from whom the entire Yoruba pantheon was born. Myth informs us that a jealous slave rolled a stone down the back of the first and only deity and shattered him in a thousand and one fragments. From this first act of revolution was born the Yoruba pantheon.

The drama which stems from this is not the drama of acting man but that of suffering spirit, the drama of Obatala. Yoruba myth syncretises Obatala, god of purity, god also of creation (but not of creativity!), with the first deity Orisa-nla. And the ritual of Obatala is a play of form, a moving celebration whose nearest equivalent in the European idiom is the Passion play. The drama is all essence: captivity, suffering and redemption. Obatala is symbolically captured, confined and ransomed. At every stage he is the embodiment of the suffering spirit of man, uncomplaining, agonised, full of the redemptive qualities of endurance and martyrdom. The music that accompanies the rites of Obatala is all clear tone and winnowed lyric, of order and harmony, stately and saintly. Significantly, the motif is white for transparency of heart and mind; there is a rejection of mystery; tones of vesture and music combine to banish mystery and terror; the poetry of the song is litanic, the dramatic idiom is the processional or ceremonial. It is a drama in which the values of conflict or the revolutionary spirit are excluded, attesting in their place the adequacy and certainty of a harmonious resolution which belongs in time and human faith. It is antithetical to the tragic challenge of Ogun in man.

Proportion in tragedy is governed by an element of the unknown in the forces of opposition or by a miscalculation by the tragic victim of such powers. The drama of Obatala dispenses with the effect of the unknown, and his agony is an evocation of the loneliness of the first deity, for this drama is, as we have stated, all pathos. And the essence is the emotional prelude to the creation of man, the limited, serene aesthetics of moulding man, not to be compared to the cosmic eruption within consciousness brought about by the re-creation of the self. The sympathetic need to be redeemed by evidence of love and human contact, by extension of the self into recognisable entities and other units of potential consciousness – this is the province of Obatala, the delicate shell of the original fullness. The profounder aspect of self-recreation, the anguish of the Will, is the portion of original restoration which has been left to the peculiar talents of Ogun, and the statement of Yoruba tragic rites is the complement of his Will to the essence of anguish. The latter by itself is crystallised in the Passion play. The drama of Obatala is prelude, suffering and aftermath. It symbolises firstly the god's unbearable loneliness and next, the memory of his incompleteness, the missing essence. And so it is also with the other gods who did not avail themselves, as did Ogun, of the chance for a redemptive combat where each might recreate each by submission to a disintegrating process within the matrix of cosmic creativity, whence the Will performs the final reassemblage. The weightiest burden of severance is that of each from self, not of godhead from mankind, and the most perilous aspect of the god's journey is that in which the deity must truly undergo the experience of transition. It is a look into the very heart of the phenomena. To fashion a bridge across it was not only Ogun's task but his very nature, and he had first to experience, to surrender his individuation once again (the first time, as a part of the original Orisa-nla Oneness) to the fragmenting process; to be resorbed within universal Oneness, the Unconscious, the deep black whirlpool of mythopoeic forces, to immerse himself thoroughly within it, understand its nature and yet by the combative value of the will to rescue and re-assemble himself and emerge wiser, powerful from the draught of cosmic secrets, organising the mystic and the technical forces of earth and cosmos to forge a bridge for his companions to follow.

It is true that to understand, to understand profoundly, is to be unnerved, deprived of the will to act. For is not human reality dwarfed by the awe and wonder, the inevitability of this cosmic gulf? It must be remembered that within this abyss are the activities of birth, death and resorption in phenomena (for the abyss is the transition between the various stages of existence). Life, the paltry reflection of the forces of the matrix, becomes suddenly inadequate, patronising and undignified when the source of creative and destructive energies is glimpsed. Suffering cancels the opaque pleasure of human existence; suffering, the truly overwhelming suffering of Sango, of Lear, of Oedipus, this suffering hones the psyche to a finely self-annihilating perceptiveness and renders further action futile and, above all, lacking in dignity. And what has the struggle of the tragic hero been, after all, but an effort to maintain that innate concept of dignity which impels to action only to that degree in which the hero possesses a true nobility of spirit? At such moments he is close to the acceptance and wisdom of Obatala in which faith is rested, not on the self, but on a universal selfhood to which individual contributions are fundamentally meaningless. It is the faith of 'knowing', the enigmatic wisdom of spiritual serenity. It is this which is often narrowly interpreted as the philosophy of the African. But philosophies are the result of primal growth and formative experience; the oracular wisdom of a race based on and continually acted upon by the collective experience of the past, present and unborn (prognostic) realities, complements the intuitive glimpse and memory of the heart of transitional being.

Yoruba 'classical' art is mostly an expression of the Obatala resolution and human beneficence, utterly devoid, on the surface, of conflict and irruption. The masks alone occasionally suggest a correspondence to the chthonic realm and hint at the archetypes of transition, yet even the majority of them flee the full power of cosmic vision, take refuge in deliberately grotesque and comic attitudes. Such distortions are easily recognised as the technique of evasion from the fullness of numinous powers. Terror is both contained by art in tragic form and released by art through comic presentation and sexual ambience. The tragic mask, however, also functions from the same source as its music – from the archetypal essences whose language derives not from the plane of physical reality or ancestral memory (the ancestor is no more than agent or medium), but from the numinous territory of transition into which the artist obtains fleeting glimpses by ritual, sacrifice and a patient submission of rational awareness to the moment when fingers and voice relate the symbolic language of the cosmos. The deft, luminous peace of Yoruba religious art blinds us therefore to the darker powers of the tragic art into which only the participant can truly enter. The grotesquerie of the terror cults misleads the unwary into equating fabricated fears with the exploration of the Yoruba mind into the mystery of his individual will and the intimations of divine suffering to which artistic man is prone. Ifa's cycle of masonic poetry – curative, prognostic, aesthetic and omniscient – expresses a philosophy of optimism in its oracular adaptiveness and unassailable resolution of all phenomena; the gods are accommodating and embrace within their eternal presences manifestations which are seemingly foreign or contradictory. It is no wonder therefore that the overt optimistic nature of the total culture is the quality attributed to the Yoruba himself, one which has began to affect his accommodation towards the modern world, a spiritual complacency with which he encounters threats to his human and unique validation. Alas, in spite of himself, from time to time, the raw urgent question beats in the blood of his temples demanding, what is the will of Ogun? For the hammering of the Yoruba will was done at Ogun's forge, and any threat of disjunction is, as with the gods, a memory code for the resurrection of the tragic myth.

Yoruba morality has also contributed to the mistaken exclusion of tragic myth from present consciousness; for, as always, the placid surface of the process of healing for spiritual or social rupture is mistaken for the absence of the principles of psychic experience that went into the restoration. Morality for the Yoruba is that which creates harmony in the cosmos, and reparation for disjunction within the individual psyche cannot be seen as compensation for the individual accident to that personality. Thus good and evil are not measured in terms of offences against the individual or even the physical community, for there is knowledge from within the corpus of Ifa oracular wisdoms that a rupture is often simply one aspect of the destructive–creative unity, that offences even against nature may be part of the exaction by deeper nature from humanity of acts which alone can open up the deeper springs of man and bring about a constant rejuvenation of the human spirit. Nature in turn benefits by such broken taboos, just as the cosmos does by demands made upon its will by man's cosmic affronts. Such acts of hubris compel the cosmos to delve deeper into its essence to meet the human challenge. Penance and retribution are not therefore aspects of punishment for crime but the first acts of a resumed awareness, an invocation of the principle of cosmic adjustment. Tragic fate is the repetitive cycle of the taboo in nature, the karmic act of hubris witting or unwitting, into which the demonic will within man constantly compels him. Powerful tragic drama follows upon the act of hubris, and myth exacts this attendant penalty from the hero where he has actually emerged victor of a conflict. Sango's taboo is based on an elementary form of hubris. Over-reaching even beyond the generous toleration due to a monarch, he fell victim to a compulsion for petty intriguing which finally led to his downfall. A final, desperate invocation of unnatural strength gave him temporary ascendancy and he routed his disloyal men. Then came the desecration of nature in which he spilt the blood of his kin. Ogun not only dared to look into transitional essence but triumphantly bridged it with knowledge, with art, with vision and the mystic creativity of science – a total and profound hubristic assertiveness that is beyond any parallel in Yoruba experience. The penalty came later when, as a reward and acknowledgement of his leadership of the divinities, gods and humans joined to offer him a crown. At first he declined but later he consented to the throne of Ire. At the first battle the same demonic energies were aroused but this was no world womb, no chthonic lair, no playground of cosmic monsters, nor could the divisions between man and man, between I and you, friend and foe, be perceived by the erstwhile hero of the transitional abyss. Enemy and subjects fell alike until Ogun alone was left, sole survivor of the narrowness of human separation. The battle is symbolic of tragic hindsight common alike to god and man. In the Ogun Mysteries this drama is a 'Passion' of a different kind, released into quietist wisdom, a ritual exorcism of demonic energies. There is no elation, not even at the end of purgation, nothing like the beatified elation of Obatala after his redemption, only a world-weariness on the rock-shelf of Promethean shoulders, a profound sorrow in the chanting of the god's recessional.[7]

Once we recognise, to revert to his Hellenic equation, the Dionysian–Apollonian–Promethean essence of Ogun, the element of hubris is seen as innate to his tragic

[7] In contemporary (public) festivals of Ogun the usual intermingling of idioms has occurred – the ritual dismembering of a surrogate dog, enactment of the massacre at Ire, the dispute between Sango and Ogun, Ogun's battle triumphs etc. The note is summatively festive.

being, requiring definition in Yoruba terms, taking it to its cyclic resolution of man's metaphysical situation. Of the profound anguish of Dionysos, the mythic disintegration of his origin is the now familiar cause, and the process of the will, no less, is what rescues the ecstatic god from being, literally, scattered to the cosmic winds. The will of Zeus is as conceptually identifiable with that of Dionysos as the elemental fragmentation of Orisa-nla can be recognised as the recurrent consciousness within Ogun (and other gods) of this kernel of terror of a previous rendering. Ripped in pieces at the hands of the titans for the (by him) unwilled acts of hubris, a divine birth, Dionysos–Zagreus commences divine existence by this experience of the destruction of the self, the transitional horror. For it is an act of hubris not only to dare the gulf of transition but to mingle essences for extra measure. We approach, it seems, the ultimate pessimism of existence as pronounced by Nietzsche's sage Silenus: it is an act of hubris to be born. It is a challenge to the jealous chthonic powers, to *be*. The answer of the Yoruba to this is just as clear: it is no less an act of hubris to *die*. And the whirlpool of transition requires both hubristic complements as catalyst to its continuous regeneration. This is the serene wisdom and essential art of Obatala. All acts are subordinate to these ultimates of the human condition and recreative will. To dare transition is the ultimate test of the human spirit, and Ogun is the first protagonist of the abyss.

The Phrygian god and his twin Ogun exercise irresistible fascination. Dionysos' thyrsus is physically and functionally paralleled by the *opa Ogun* borne by the male devotees of Ogun. But the thyrsus of Dionysos is brighter; it is all light and running wine, Ogun's stave is more symbolic of his labours through the night of transition. A long willowy pole, it is topped by a frond-bound lump of ore which strains the pole in wilful curves and keeps it vibrant. The bearers, who can only be men, are compelled to move about among the revellers as the effort to keep the ore-head from toppling over keeps them perpetually on the move. Through town and village, up the mountain to the grove of Ogun this dance of the straining phallus-heads pocks the air above men and women revellers who are decked in palm fronds and bear palm branches in their hands. A dog is slaughtered in sacrifice, and the mock-struggle of the head priest and his acolytes for the carcass, during which it is literally torn limb from limb, inevitably brings to mind the dismemberment of Zagreus, son of Zeus. Most significant of all is the brotherhood of the palm and the ivy. The mystery of the wine of palm, bled straight from the tree and potent without further ministration, is a miracle of nature acquiring symbolic significance in the Mysteries of Ogun. For it was instrumental in the tragic error of the god and his sequent Passion. Like Obatala also, the gods commit their error after an excess of the potent draught. Ogun was full of wine before his battle at the head of the Ire army. After his dark deed, the wine fog slowly lifted and he was left with nothing but dread truth. Obatala, moulder of men, fell also to the fumes of wine; his craftsman's fingers lost their control and he moulded cripples, albinos, the blind and other deformed. Obatala the eternal penitent therefore forbids wine to his worshippers in or out of his seasonal rites while Ogun, in proud acceptance of the need to create a challenge for the constant exercise of will and control, enjoins the liberal joy of wine. The palm fronds are a symbol of his wilful, ecstatic being.

And how else may the inhibiting bonds of man be dissolved when he goes to meet his god, how else may he quickly enter into the god's creative being, or his inner ear and eye respond to the fleeting presences which guard the abode of gods, how else partake in the psychic revelry of the world when it celebrates a crossing of the abyss of non-being? The sculpted rites of the worship of Obatala are rapturous also, but lacking in ecstasy. It is a dance of amelioration to tyrannic powers, not a celebration of the infinite will of the Promethean spirit. The one is withdrawal, the other an explosion of the forces of darkness and joy, explosion of the sun's kernel, an eruption of fire which is the wombfruit of pristine mountains, for no less, no different were the energies within Ogun whose ordering and control through the will brought him safely through the tragic gulf. Even through the medium of this ecstasy, a glimpse is obtained of the vastness of the abyss; the true devotee knows, understands and penetrates the god's anguish. In the centre of the swaying, milling, ecstatic horde where his individuation is routed and he submits to a union of joy, the inner being encounters the precipice. Poised on the heights of the physical mountain-home of Ogun he experiences a yawning gulf within him, a menacing maul of chthonic strength yawning ever wider to annihilate his being; he is saved only by channelling the dark torrent into the plastic light of poetry and dance; not, however, as a reflection or illusion of reality, but as the celebrative aspects of the resolved crisis of his god.

Index

Abrahams, Peter, 65
Achebe, Chinua, 87–8, 92–5
  Arrow of God: Christianity in,
    88, 89, 90, 96; Ezeulu, 87,
    88, 89, 90, 91, 92–6; politics
    in, 88, 92, 94; secular nature
    of, 87; quoted, 87, 88, 89–92
    passim, 93, 94–5 *passim*
acting, and the tragic spirit, 146
actor
  Ogun, the first a., 142, 145,
    149–50
  in ritual drama, 30, 32, 36; as
    mouthpiece of the god, 30,
    143; in Ogun Mysteries,
    142–3
African (The), *see* Conton
African world view
  accommodative nature of,
    53–4, 54n
  in *Breath*, 131–4
  and creative separatism, 130
  in *Dark Child (The)*, 122
  and drama, 37–60
  and moral order, 52–3
  pre-colonial, 100, 105–6,
    112–13, 115, 138–9
  in *Radiance of the King (The)*,
    123–5
  and 'religion', 122
Ambiguous Adventure, *see* Kane
American progressive theatre, 6,
  7
ancestors, 4, 10, 18, 26, 144, 148,
  149
Aninta, god of, 95, 96
Anyanya insurrection, 109
apartheid, 69, 71; *see also* South
  Africa

Apollo
  and Obatala, 140–1
  and Ogun, 26, 141
Arab–Islamic colonisation of
  black Africa, 100, 104–8
Armah, Ayi Kwei, 86, 106–7,
  109–16, 120, 121
  *Beautyful Ones are Not Yet
    Born (The)*, 116
  Two Thousand Seasons: and
    Arab–Islamic colonialism,
    106–7; and monarchy, 113;
    secular vision of, 114–15;
    sexual themes in, 110–11;
    vengeance motif in, 110;
    violence in, 114–15; and 'the
    way', 112; weaknesses of,
    114; quoted, 107, 110–11,
    114, 115
Arrow of God, *see* Achebe
Aryan myth, 102–3, 142
Atunda, 27
audience
  European, reaction to *Song of
    a Goat*, 45, 46
  and European theatre:
    medieval, 40–1; modern, 41
  and Greek theatre, 40
  participation of, 38–9
  and ritual theatre, 33–4, 41–3

Ba, Hampate
  *Tierno Bokar, le Sage de
    Bandiagara*, 77–8; quoted,
    78
Bacchae (The), 7, 12
  quoted, 12–13
Bahia, 16, 17, 18
Baldwin, James, 103, 104

161

Index

Index